Struggle for the Shenandoah

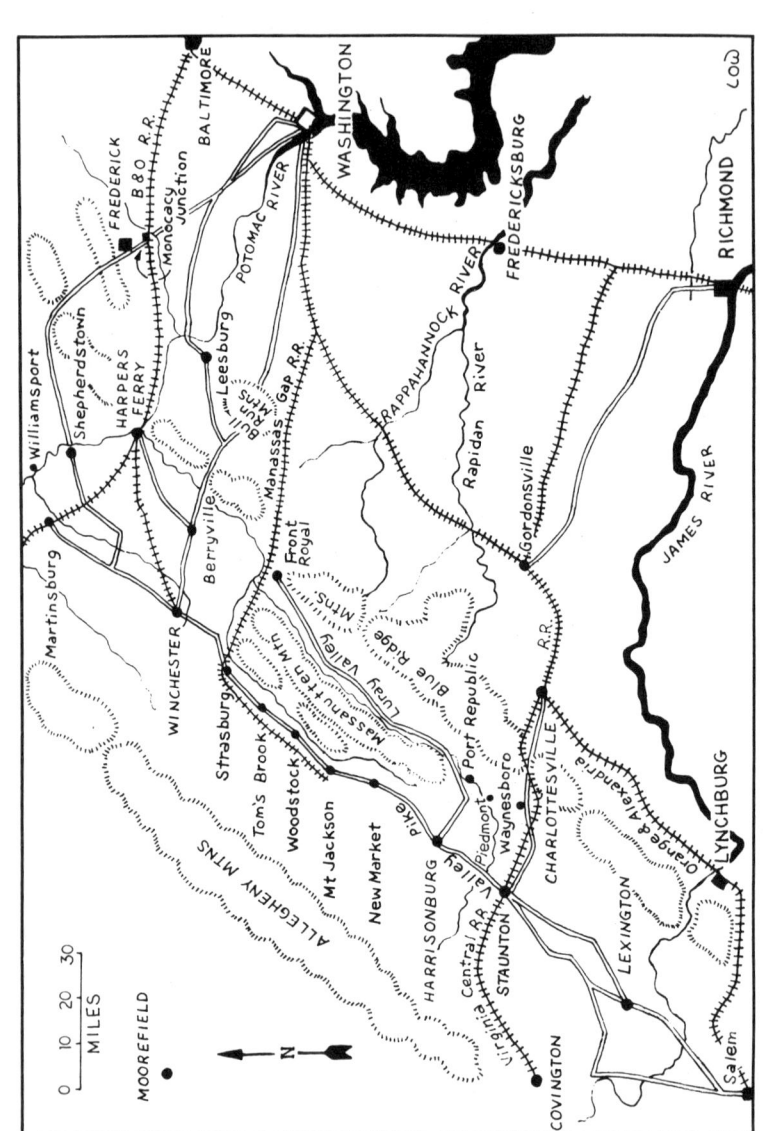

Theater of Operations, June–October 1864

STRUGGLE

FOR THE

SHENANDOAH

Essays on the 1864 Valley Campaign

EDITED BY
Gary W. Gallagher

THE KENT STATE UNIVERSITY PRESS
Kent, Ohio, and London, England

© 1991 by The Kent State University Press, Kent, Ohio 44242
Library of Congress Catalog Card Number 90–47368
ISBN 0–87338–429–6
ISBN 0–87338–430–X (pbk.)
Manufactured in the United States of America

03 02 01 00 99 98   5 4 3 2

Library of Congress Cataloging-in-Publication Data

Struggle for the Shenandoah : essays on the 1864 valley campaign /
edited by Gary W. Gallagher.
    p. cm.
Includes bibliographical references (p.) and index.
Contents: The Shenandoah Valley in 1864 / Gary W. Gallagher —
Jubal A. Early and confederate leadership / Jeffry D. Wert — Union
generalship in the 1864 valley campaign / A. Wilson Greene — "The
cause of all my disasters" : Jubal A. Early and the undisciplined
valley cavalry / Robert K. Krick — "I resolved to play a bold
game" : John S. Mosby as a factor in the 1864 valley campaign /
Dennis E. Frye.
ISBN 0–87338–429–6 (cloth : alk.) ∞ — ISBN 0–87338–430–X
(pbk. : alk.) ∞
    1. Shenandoah Valley Campaign, 1864 (May–August) 2. Shenandoah
Valley Campaign, 1864 (August–November) I. Gallagher, Gary W.
E476.66.S77 1991
973.7'37—dc20   90–47368
                                                            CIP

British Library Cataloging-in-Publication data are available.

Contents

Introduction

GARY W. GALLAGHER

common perception of military events in Virginia following Ulysses S. Grant's campaign from the Wilderness to
Petersburg focuses on armies hunkered behind formidable
entrenchments. Even casual students of the Civil War know
about Robert E. Lee's oft-expressed fear of being trapped in
the works of Richmond and Petersburg. Once denied the mobility that had enabled him to thwart a series of Federal commanders in 1862 and 1863, Lee argued that a siege inevitably
would lead to Northern victory. Despite this pessimistic out-
look, he mounted an effective defense of the Southern capital
for more than nine grinding months, surviving a close call at
the Battle of the Crater in late July 1864 and launching several
limited offensives in an effort to break Grant's tenacious grip.
Lee's last aggressive spasm during the protracted siege came
in late March 1865 at Fort Stedman, where several thousand
Confederate casualties gained no advantage. Within a week,
the Battle of Five Forks and Grant's final assaults at Petersburg
settled the question. Only the long retreat toward Appomattox
remained before the war in Virginia drew to a merciful close.

Many writers point to the stalemate along the Richmond-
Petersburg front from July 1864 to April 1865 as a precursor of
twentieth-century warfare. Look to Virginia in the final year of
the Civil War, they argue, to find a preview of the hideous
Western Front of World War I. Photographs of the maze of
Union and Confederate trenches, bombproofs, forts, and impressive siege weaponry lend visual support to the notion that
the war reached a grim impasse once the armies crossed the
James River in June 1864.

An understanding of the conflict's greatest siege, however, falls considerably short of providing the whole picture in

Virginia. Far to the northwest, while the soldiers of Grant and Lee methodically extended their ugly slashes of earthworks, armies waged a highly complex, dramatic, and important campaign in the beautiful Shenandoah Valley. From mid-June 1864 until the end of the year, events in the Valley frequently held the attention of the political and military leadership of both sides. Civilians also looked eagerly for news from the Shenandoah, where rapidly changing circumstances offered fluid counterpoint to the immobile forces outside Richmond. A side show in the beginning, when Grant assigned the inept Franz Sigel and a relative handful of troops to the region, campaigning in the Shenandoah built to a turbulent crescendo. The Valley became a true second front, involving nearly seventy-five thousand combatants and encompassing most of the military action in Virginia.

Those who seek evidence of modern war in the lines at Petersburg might just as profitably look to the Valley in 1864. If Grant and Lee anticipated one variety of twentieth-century conflict, the confrontation between Jubal A. Early and Philip H. Sheridan foreshadowed others. The 1864 Valley campaign included large doses of the type of rapid movement punctuated by bitter battles that would reappear in the freewheeling action in Europe during World War II. It also witnessed the first broad application of Grant's strategy of exhaustion, which inflicted on civilians in the Valley the sort of wholesale destruction of property all too familiar in modern warfare. Finally, a bitter element of guerrilla activity added dark texture to the campaign; bushwhacking, reprisals, summary executions, and punishment of civilians who harbored partisans created a violent mosaic common to twentieth-century guerrilla conflicts.

Two men stood at the center of the 1864 Valley campaign. Jubal A. Early took a large part of Lee's army and the high hopes of his commander with him to the Shenandoah in June 1864. Eventually Early and his men would march more than sixteen hundred miles, fight dozens of battles and skirmishes, reach the outskirts of Washington, D.C., and compel Lincoln and Grant to divert considerable resources to end Confederate military activity in the Valley and destroy the region's logistical capacity. As a leading postwar architect of the Lost Cause explanation for Southern defeat, Early emphasized that over-whelming Northern advantages of men and material spelled doom for the Confederacy. This simplistic argument ignored a range of factors that contributed to Confederate failure; how-ever, in the case of the Valley in 1864, Early's emphasis on numbers had great validity. Facing Federal armies three times the size of his own, Early had scant margin for error. He gen-erally performed at a high level, but every mistake cost him dearly. In the end, he suffered catastrophic failure, lost the Valley, and incurred the unforgiving wrath of the Confederate people.

Sheridan's experience in the Valley propelled him to the first rank of Union heroes. Enjoying only lukewarm support from key Northern leaders in the beginning, he answered all doubts with a string of impressive successes at Third Winchester, Fisher's Hill, and Cedar Creek. Sheridan blundered on several occasions, quarreled with subordinates, and displayed an odd timidity at one crucial point in the campaign. Only his pre-ponderant strength enabled him to recover from shaky starts at Third Winchester and Cedar Creek. But the bottom line left no room for quibbling: his capacity to build an army, instill high morale among its soldiers, and inspire troops in battle through superb personal leadership resulted in overwhelming triumph. The Northern populace cared nothing about nitpicking criti-cisms of Sheridan's generalship. They counted the victories and warmly embraced Grant's young lieutenant. Abraham Lincoln shared this enthusiasm for Sheridan because the Valley campaign—together with William Tecumseh Sherman's capture of Atlanta and David G. Farragut's victory at Mobile Bay—virtually assured Republican majorities in the November 1864 elections.

The 1864 Valley campaign exceeded in scale and importance Stonewall Jackson's more famous 1862 operations in the Shenandoah. Yet it has never generated equal enthusiasm among students of the Civil War. A conference held in 1989 at the Mont Alto campus of Pennsylvania State University exam-ined the 1864 Valley campaign from several angles. Where did it fit into the larger military framework of the war? What is a fair assessment of Early and Sheridan? Was the result inevitable in light of the disparity of resources? What role did John S. Mosby and his Confederate guerrillas play? The essays printed herein represent revised versions of papers delivered at the Mont Alto conference. They offer neither a detailed tactical analysis of the campaign nor a consensus on all major questions. The authors do agree that events in the Shenandoah Valley loomed very large during the crucial second half of 1864, and they hope their essays will spark further interest in the subject.

The Mont Alto Conferences on the Civil War always bring together a congenial group of historians and participants. Bob Krick, Will Greene, Jeff Wert, and Dennis Frye supplied a wealth of information and insight leavened with good humor. They also met deadlines, an attribute often missing in otherwise admirable personalities. Their cheerful cooperation made this book possible. Thomas A. Low graciously agreed to prepare the maps despite a most unreasonable timetable imposed by the editor (the ghost of Jed Hotchkiss no doubt stood at Tom's shoulder during the ordeal). Eileen Anne Gallagher once again turned often sloppy pages into a clean manuscript. She did so despite a visceral aversion to Philip H. Sheridan, who, she believes, is an embarrassment to all people of Irish descent. The agony of typing Sheridan's name innumerable times took its toll, but she persevered in stalwart fashion. I am much indebted to all of these people for their work on this project.

Struggle for the Shenandoah

The Shenandoah Valley in 1864

GARY W. GALLAGHER

Few geographical regions associated with the Civil War inspire more dramatic images than the Shenandoah Valley. Some of the images are romantic, heavily charged with the gloss of improbable Southern triumph against long odds. The figure of Thomas J. "Stonewall" Jackson towers above all others of this type, waging a bold campaign that catapulted the dour Virginian to a lofty position as the most famous soldier in the Confederacy. Just behind Jackson's exploits in any catalog of memorable scenes from the Valley come the young men of the Virginia Military Institute, who achieved their own form of immortality when they fought and died to help win the Battle of New Market in May 1864. Cast in darker hues are Philip H. Sheridan and the Federal army that brought the agony of U. S. Grant's strategy of exhaustion to the Valley during the last autumn of the war. Sheridan and his men left a legacy of blackened ruin that served as graphic counterpoint to the storied lushness of the area. From beginning to end, the Valley bore witness to events that across more than a century and a quarter continue to evoke emotional responses from students of the war.

The Shenandoah Valley cuts a fertile, rolling slash between the piedmont of Virginia and the rugged mountains of the state's antebellum western regions. A landscape of breathtaking beauty and agricultural bounty, the Valley extends from the Potomac River to beyond Lexington in Rockbridge County. Positioned between the Blue Ridge Mountains on the east and the more imposing Alleghenies to the west, the Valley runs southwest to northeast and drops gently in its course to meet the Potomac. The forks of the Shenandoah River thus flow south to north (or southwest to northeast), which means that

I

an individual traveling to the Potomac goes "down the Valley," an odd circumstance in a world where north is almost always "up." Between Strasburg and Harrisonburg the Massanutten Range divides the Valley—west of the Massanuttens, in the Valley proper, the North Fork of the Shenandoah River makes its lazy way toward the Potomac, while to the east the South Fork runs through the Luray (or Page) Valley on its journey to join the North Fork at Front Royal. The lower Valley, as the northern portion is known, includes the broad expanse between Williamsport on the Potomac and Strasburg, as well as the land west of the Massanuttens from Woodstock to Strasburg. A secondary valley parallels the northeastern flank of the lower Valley, nestling between the Blue Ridge and the modest bulk of the Bull Run Mountains and embracing parts of Loudoun and Fauquier counties. In its diverse entirety, the Valley presents a striking stage, over which Union and Confederate armies played out a series of compelling military operations during the four years of war.

The logistical importance of the Valley during the conflict scarcely can be overstated. Its agricultural riches promised sustenance for Southern forces in Virginia. The most important wheat growing area in the entire Upper South through most of the antebellum period, it also led Virginia in production of other grains and cattle and contributed substantial quantities of leather, wood products, woolen textiles, and whiskey. No rail system served the entire Valley, but three lines provided links to northern and eastern Virginia. The Virginia Central crossed the Blue Ridge into the Valley near Waynesboro and ran to Staunton and thence to Covington; the Manassas Gap Railroad linked Mount Jackson, Strasburg, and Front Royal to Manassas Junction via Thoroughfare Gap in the Bull Run Mountains. The Winchester and Potomac Railroad, a spur of the B&O, penetrated the lower Valley from Harpers Ferry to Winchester. Staunton served as the largest rail depot in the Valley, home for extensive Confederate warehouses and hospitals. Supplementing these railroads as an artery for the movement of logistical goods was the macadamized Valley Turnpike, which provided all-weather service between

Staunton and Martinsburg. The Confederacy could ill afford to neglect the defense of a region so valuable logistically, and of necessity it looked especially to guard the Virginia Central's access to this bounty of food, fodder, and other material. The Valley's importance loomed equally large as a strategic avenue whence either side might mount a threat to the western flanks of Washington or Richmond. All of the Valley below Strasburg lay north of the Federal capital. A Confederate army marching down the Valley, screened by cavalry in the gaps of the Blue Ridge, might easily cross the Potomac and descend on the right rear of Washington. The B&O Railroad lay vulnerable to Southern attack where it dipped south of the Potomac from Harpers Ferry to Martinsburg. Moreover, any Northern advance through north-central Virginia along the Orange & Alexandria Railroad would present an open right flank to Confederates lurking behind the passes of the Blue Ridge. Similarly, Federals moving up the Valley could cut the rail links to eastern Virginia, thereby disrupting the flow of supplies to the soldiers defending Richmond, while at the same time placing in jeopardy the left flank of any Southern army between the Occoquan and the Rappahannock–Rapidan River line.

Military activity in the Shenandoah Valley during the Civil War underscored the region's logistical and strategic importance. From the confrontation between Joseph E. Johnston and Robert Patterson prior to First Manassas in 1861, through the final pathetic Confederate defeat at Waynesboro on March 2, 1865, almost continuous combat of some sort violated the pastoral countryside. The Valley saw more than a dozen pitched battles, hundreds of skirmishes, and chronic guerrilla activity carried on by John S. Mosby, John H. and Jesse McNeill, Harry Gilmor, and other partisan leaders that escalated in 1864 to the point of retaliatory hangings. The Army of Northern Virginia depended on secure lines of supply through the Valley during R. E. Lee's raid into Maryland in 1862, and the following summer Confederates marched down the Valley on their way to Pennsylvania and the Battle of Gettysburg.

Two campaigns in the Shenandoah Valley stand out as the most important: those conducted by Stonewall Jackson between

March and June 1862 and by Jubal A. Early between June and
October 1864. The first grew out of R. E. Lee's belief that a
strategic diversion in the Shenandoah Valley would immobi-
lize Federal troops otherwise destined to reinforce George B.
McClellan's Army of the Potomac in its advance against Richmond. Irvin McDowell commanded about thirty-five thousand
Union troops near Fredericksburg, Nathaniel P. Banks another
fifteen to twenty thousand in the lower Valley, and John C.
Frémont about eight thousand in the Alleghenies of western
Virginia. Lee wanted Jackson to pin down Federal forces west
of the Blue Ridge, lest they join McDowell for a movement
against Richmond from the north while McClellan's one hundred thousand–man horde approached the capital from the
southeast.

Armed with Lee's strategic plan, Jackson proceeded to carry
out his broad orders in memorable fashion. In a whirlwind of
action, "Old Jack" drove his men up the Valley to defeat
part of Frémont's little army at McDowell on May 8, then
crossed the Massanuttens at New Market and marched quickly
down the Luray corridor to achieve a pair of victories at
Front Royal and Winchester on May 23 and 25. Next he withdrew to the southern terminus of the Massanutten range,
where he notched another brace of wins against Frémont and
Shields at Cross Keys and Port Republic on June 8 and 9. Having blunted the clumsy thrusts of his opponents in the Valley
and persuaded the Lincoln government to hold McDowell at
Fredericksburg, Jackson eventually slipped across the Blue
Ridge to reinforce the Southern army at Richmond. Speed,
deception, knowledge of the terrain, and willingness to take
risks paid off handsomely for Jackson at a time when the
Confederacy hungered for good news from its military forces.
After months of dreary reports of disaster in the Western
Theater, Southerners savored the good news from the Valley
and accorded Jackson frenzied acclaim as their premier mili-
tary hero.

Slightly less than two years after Jackson's victory at Port
Republic, another Federal menace appeared that would trigger
the Valley's most sustained and bloody campaigning. U. S.
Grant included the Valley in his plans for simultaneous offen-

sives in May 1864. He plotted major operations in the Western Theater, where his friend William Tecumseh Sherman would strike toward Atlanta from Chattanooga and where Nathaniel P. Banks would drive from Mobile into the interior of Alabama. In Virginia, Grant wanted the Army of the Potomac to hit the Army of Northern Virginia somewhere along the Rappahannock River frontier, bleed it as much as possible, and prevent its sending reinforcements to the West, while Benjamin F. Butler's Army of the James closed on the Confederate capital from the southeast.

In the Valley, Grant ordered Major General Franz Sigel, a native of Germany who commanded the sprawling Department of West Virginia, to move toward Staunton to distract Lee's attention. Other troops from Sigel's department would attempt to sever the rail link between Lynchburg and Tennessee. Sigel filled the least important role in Grant's grand scheme. Indeed, the general-in-chief admitted to Sherman in April 1864 that Sigel's need to guard the B&O circumscribed his offensive potential in the Valley: "With the long line of rail-road Sigel has to protect he can spare no troops except to move directly to his front. In this way he must get through to inflict great damage on the enemy, or the enemy must detach from one of his armies a large force to prevent it." Grant concluded with an image borrowed from President Lincoln: "In other words, if Sigel cant skin himself he can hold a leg whilst some one else skins."

Sigel quickly proved the wisdom of Grant's low expectations. Learning that some of Sigel's troops under W. W. Averell had broken the Virginia & Tennessee Railroad west of Lynchburg, Grant asked Chief-of-Staff Henry W. Halleck on May 17, "Cannot General Sigel go up the Shenandoah Valley toward Staunton? The enemy is evidently drawing supplies largely from that source, and if Sigel can destroy the road there, it will be of vast importance to us." Grant clearly grasped the importance of Staunton as a shipping depot, via the Virginia Central, for Valley products directed to Lee's army. But at the time Grant wrote Halleck, Sigel already had failed to capture Staunton. A political general appointed because of his influence among German voters, Sigel had advanced with an army of sixty-five hundred up the Valley as far as New Market. There he met a motley force under John C. Breckinridge that numbered among its fifty-one hundred men the battalion of cadets from the Virginia Military Institute. Hard fighting under a threatening sky resulted in a Confederate victory that propelled Sigel back toward the lower Valley. "We are doing a good business in this department," quipped a perceptive Federal staff officer. "Averell is tearing up the Virginia and Tennessee Railroad while Sigel is tearing down the Valley turnpike."

Following their victory at New Market, most of Breckinridge's soldiers traveled eastward to reinforce Lee at Richmond. Meanwhile, Grant decided to press matters in the Valley. He replaced Sigel, whom he characterized as a man "who will do nothing but run," with Major General David Hunter. Determined to deny Lee the products of the Valley's farmers and artisans, Grant instructed Hunter to move through Staunton to Charlottesville and Lynchburg "living off the country" and destroying the Virginia Central Railroad "beyond possibility of repair for weeks." Hunter went at his task with the zeal of a man who believed that the South should pay dearly for its transgressions against the Constitution and the human rights of enslaved blacks. On June 5, eighty-five hundred Federals under Hunter defeated W. E. "Grumble" Jones and fifty-five hundred Confederates at the battle of Piedmont some seven miles southwest of Port Republic (Jones himself was killed in the action). Staunton fell almost immediately, after which Hunter proceeded up the Valley to Lexington, where he burned the Virginia Military Institute on June 11. Increasingly, Hunter's men also laid a heavy hand on civilian property of all kinds.

Anger welled among civilians in the Valley who tasted the bitter fruit of total warfare that would soon engulf large sections of Virginia and the South. Word of Hunter's actions spread quickly across the Confederacy, prompting a woman in North Carolina to note angrily in her diary that the Federals "have no supplies, no waggons, & live off the country, pillaging, robbing, & committing the most horrible outrages." Those closer to the scene poured out far more vitriol. Henrietta Lee, wife of a cousin of R. E. Lee whose house and outbuildings were put to the torch, promised Hunter that the "curses of thousands, the scorn of the manly and upright and the hatred of the true and honorable, will follow you and yours through all time, and brand your name *infamy.* INFAMY."

Lee and Jefferson Davis watched Hunter's progress with growing alarm. On June 6, Lee conceded the possibility that Hunter "will do us great evil" in the Valley but resisted detachment of any troops from the Army of Northern Virginia except those that had come with Breckinridge after New Market. Reports from the Valley over the next week suggested to Davis, at least, that the Federals meant "to destroy all communications with Richmond" from the west and south and "thus to compel the evacuation of the capital." Hunter's principal target appeared to be Lynchburg, a center for hospitals, communications, and rail and canal transportation. Davis apparently pressed Lee to send troops to protect Lynchburg, prompting the general to acknowledge "the advantage of expelling the enemy from the Valley." But it would take a corps to do the job, added Lee. "If it is deemed prudent to hazard the defense of Richmond . . . I will do so," concluded the reluctant general. "I think this is what the enemy would desire." In the end, Lee decided to send Jubal A. Early and the Second Corps to Lynchburg.

The decision reflected Lee's audacious personality. Never one to employ half-measures, he tapped his best corps commander (James Longstreet was recuperating from a wound) and Stonewall Jackson's old corps to carry out a diversionary operation reminiscent of the 1862 Valley campaign. "Finding that it would be necessary to detach some troops to repel the force under General Hunter, which was threatening Lynchburg," Lee explained to the secretary of war, "I resolved to send one that would be adequate to accomplish that purpose effectually, and, if possible, strike a decisive blow." Early's immediate task was the relief of Lynchburg. Should Hunter retreat down the Valley, Early was to follow him, free the Valley of Union troops, cross the Potomac to menace Washington and Baltimore, and perhaps compel Grant to reinforce the national capital at the expense of the Army of the Potomac, which

Lieutenant General Jubal Anderson Early

might then be driven from Richmond. Lee conveyed all of this to Early on the evening of June 12. The next morning the troops were on the march, and when they turned west, away from Richmond, some of the veterans suspected they were bound for the Great Valley of Virginia, scene of so many Southern triumphs two years earlier.

Early moved his troops rapidly to Lynchburg, reaching the city on July 17 as Hunter edged toward its outer defenses. The Confederates repulsed probing attacks on June 18. Hunter's depredations engendered within the Southern ranks an unusually bitter resolve to chastise the enemy. Early shared the feelings of his men—as well as open disdain for the second-line Southern cavalry that had been contesting the Union advance—and at one juncture took position along the front lines, raised himself in his stirrups, shook a fist at the Federals, and shouted: "No buttermilk rangers after you now, you Goddamned Blue Butts!" Though his army outnumbered Early's by a few thousand men, Hunter believed that he faced a superior enemy and thus elected to withdraw on June 19 rather than attempt to fight his way into Lynchburg. Hastening toward western Virginia just ahead of pursuing Confederates, the Federals reached safety in the rugged Alleghenies west of Salem. There Hunter reviewed his campaign, judging it, with some justification, "extremely successful, inflicting great injury upon the enemy" with the destruction of transportation and other property. Early broke off pursuit on June 21, rested his troops the next day at Botetourt Springs northeast of Salem, and prepared to implement the second phase of Lee's instructions.

The newly christened Confederate Army of the Valley marched northward on June 23. Moving swiftly, it swept the Valley clean of Federals and on July 5 and 6 crossed the Potomac into Maryland. Looping north and then east across South Mountain and the Catoctins, skirmishing as it went, the Army of the Valley defeated a small force under Lew Wallace at the Battle of the Monocacy below Frederick, Maryland, on July 9. The road to Washington now lay open. On July 10, weary Southern infantrymen struggled forward along dust-choked roads in oppressive heat, with Early and his leading units arriving at the outskirts of Washington on July 11.

A degree of alarm permeated Northern efforts to cope with this unexpected Southern raid. Always extremely sensitive about the safety of the capital, the War Department issued calls for twenty-four thousand militia from New York and Pennsylvania. "The President has been a good deal incredulous about a very large army north of the Potomac," Secretary of the Navy Gideon Welles recorded in his diary on July 7, "yet he begins to manifest anxiety." The next day Welles described Lincoln as "enjoined to silence, while Halleck is in a perfect maze, without intelligent decision or self-reliance, and [Secretary of War Edwin M.] Stanton is wisely ignorant." Assistant Secretary of War Charles A. Dana traveled from Grant's headquarters to Washington on July 11, finding a vacuum of leadership in which "General Halleck would not give orders, except as he received them from Grant; the President would give none; and . . . everything was practically at a standstill."

Lincoln evinced mild panic in a telegram to Grant on July 10. The militia from New York and Pennsylvania "will [be] scarcely worth counting," argued the president. Troops at Harpers Ferry were "not very reliable"; Hunter remained far to Early's rear; and Wallace's command, including James B. Ricketts's division of the Sixth Corps that Grant had dispatched to help stop Early, "was so badly beaten yesterday at Monocacy, that what is left can attempt no more than to defend Baltimore." Lincoln closed with a suggestion that Grant leave enough of the Army of the Potomac to hold the lines opposite Lee "and bring the rest with you personally, and make a vigorous effort to destroy the enemie's force in this vicinity." Aware of waning enthusiasm among Northern civilians to prosecute the war, as well as growing disenchantment among Democrats and some Republicans with his administration's policies, Lincoln clearly believed that Grant's presence would prevent a disaster at Washington that might cost him his office and forestall restoration of the Union.

Grant declined to divert his main attention from Petersburg to Washington. "I have sent from here a whole corps commanded by an excellent officer [Horatio G. Wright and the Sixth Corps]," Grant assured Lincoln on the evening of July 10, "besides over three thousand other troops." A division of the Nineteenth Corps followed close behind, and "before more troops can be sent from here Hunter will be able to join Wright in rear of the Enemy, with at least ten thousand men." His departure from Petersburg prior to achieving victory on that front would signal failure, thought Grant, exacerbating the already serious decline in Northern morale. On the morning of July 11, with gunfire audible from the direction of Rockville, Maryland, a calmer Lincoln indicated that Grant's dispositions seemed "very satisfactory." The president hoped that Wright and Hunter could unite to hit the Confederates before they reached the fords over the Potomac.

The military drama north of Washington rushed to a conclusion on July 11 and 12. While Early's infantry probed the formidable works ringing the Federal capital, Southern intelligence brought word that elements of the Sixth Corps had bolstered the defending garrison. Other Union units reportedly approached from the northwest. This information and consultation with his divisional commanders convinced Early that he lacked the strength to punch through the defenses into Washington. The day's delay at the Monocacy, which afforded Grant time to get veterans to Washington by July 11, had proved decisive. The Army of the Valley remained in front of Washington for two days—in the course of which Lincoln rode out to the works and came under fire—before withdrawing unmolested to the lower Valley via White's Ford between July 13 and 15.

The first phase of the 1864 Valley campaigning ended with Early's return to Virginia. Although some Southerners perceived the operation as a failure because Washington remained in Federal hands, Early had accomplished everything on Lee's agenda. Lynchburg was safe, the Valley free of Yankees, and Grant had weakened the Army of the Potomac to buttress the defense of Washington. "Old Jube" also fed his army on the move and protected the coming harvest in the Valley. Lee informed the secretary of war that "so far as the movement was intended to relieve our territory in that section of the enemy, it has up to the present time been successful." "The value of the results obtained need not be further stated," added Lee in a sentence that underscored his confidence in Early, "as there are yet some to be expected in the future."

Many of Early's soldiers complained of an absence of sufficient appreciation for their efforts. Dodson Ramseur, who led Early's old division, testily noticed that "the Richmond papers are 'pitching into' Gen'l Early for not taking Washington." Had Early attempted it, thought Ramseur, "he would have been repulsed with great loss, and then these same wiseacres would have condemned him for recklessness." Early himself subsequently stressed that Lee "did not expect that I would be able to capture Washington . . . he only expected me to threaten the city and cause the withdrawal of troops from Grant's army." Perhaps the best expression of the spirit that animated the raid across the Potomac also came from Early, who remarked to Henry Kyd Douglas as the army began its march back to Virginia, "Major, we haven't taken Washington, but we've scared Abe Lincoln like h[ell]!"

The impact of Early's raid north of the Potomac in fact extended well beyond Lincoln. A Northern populace already pessimistic because of endless casualties in Virginia and an absence of good news from Sherman in north Georgia found it hard to believe that Rebels had skirted the suburbs of Washington and escaped unharmed. A New York diarist recorded on July 9 rumors that Confederates occupied Frederick and were likely to march on Baltimore, admitting that he was "sick and sore with long anxiety about the war." Attorney General Edward Bates lashed out on July 14 against "the impotence and treachery of our military rulers! The raiders have retired across the Potomac, with all their booty safe! Nobody seems disposed to hinder them." Some soldiers in the Army of the Potomac used Early's campaign to vent anger against lukewarm civilian support for the war. "Here in the army we look upon this raid as a good thing," Robert McAllister wrote his family on July 16. For too long, thought this soldier, the Northern people had pursued money rather than look to the national safety: "These Rebel raids stirs the people up and shows them the necessity of immediate action. Now things will go on right again."

Early's bold movements through the rest of July convinced Grant and Lincoln to commit substantial Federal resources to deny the Confederacy use of the Valley as either a bread-basket or an avenue of strategic advance. On July 24, the Army of the Valley defeated Federals under George H. Crook near Winchester in the Battle of Second Kernstown. Six days later some of Early's cavalry under John McCausland burned Chambersburg, Pennsylvania, in retaliation for Hunter's actions in the Valley, while Southern infantry skirmished with Union units near Emmitsburg and Monocacy Junction, Maryland. Forays against the B&O by Confederate cavalry and guerrillas continued through July and into August. By the end of July, Grant had seen enough. He directed that Wright's Sixth Corps, William H. Emory's Nineteenth Corps (recently arrived from Louisiana) as well as the forces of the Department of West Virginia be placed under Philip H. Sheridan. Sheridan would command the new Middle Division encompassing Northern Virginia, Washington, West Virginia, Maryland, and Pennsylvania.

Grant hoped that Sheridan could defeat Early "and follow him to the death," but his primary focus was logistical. Without food from the Valley, Lee's army at Petersburg would suffer crippling shortages. Consequently, Grant ordered Sheridan to give "the enemy no rest, and if it is possible to follow to the Virginia Central road. . . . Do all the damage to railroads and crops you can. Carry off stock of all descriptions, and negroes, so as to prevent further planting. . . . If the war is to last another year," added Grant in words that bespoke a grim shift to his strategy of exhaustion aimed at destroying the logistical base of the Confederate war effort, "we want the Shenandoah Valley to remain a barren waste." This deployment of Sheridan and a force that would climb to more than fifty thousand men signaled Grant's determination to open a massive second front in Virginia—a front rivaling in importance that at Petersburg. Lee countered by directing Early to remain in the Valley, both to divert as much strength as possible from the Army of the Potomac and to secure the fall harvest.

The climactic phase of the war in the Valley commenced in the first week of August. Following a period during which Early and Sheridan played cat-and-mouse in the lower

Major General Philip Henry Sheridan

Valley, campaigning built to a bloody crescendo between mid-September and mid-October. The Federals inaugurated their offensive on September 19 at Third Winchester, pummeling the

Confederates late in the afternoon after a morning of stubborn fighting. Three days later, at Fisher's Hill just above Strasburg, Sheridan's soldiers routed Early's demoralized men a second time. Following this defeat, Early retreated to Rockfish Gap, leaving the Valley from Harrisonburg northward at the mercy of the Federal Army of the Shenandoah. Sheridan tracked Early at leisure, systematically destroying crops, barns, mills, and livestock as far south as Harrisonburg and Port Republic. As columns of dense black smoke billowed skyward across large stretches of the Valley, Sheridan detected a waning Southern resolve. "The peopole here are getting sick of the war," he wrote Grant from Woodstock on October 7. "The whole country . . . has been made untenable for a rebel army. . . . This destruction embraces the Luray Valley and Little Fort Valley [on Massanutten Mountain], as well as the main valley." Sheridan conceded, however, that problems with transportation rendered a movement against the railroad at Charlottesville impossible. "The best policy," he thought, "will be to let the burning of the crops of the Valley be the end of this campaign, and let some of this army go somewhere else."

When Sheridan retraced his steps down the Valley the second week in October, Early shadowed him to the vicinity of Middletown. On October 19, the Confederates delivered a brilliant surprise attack at Cedar Creek that routed two-thirds of the much larger Federal army. Hesitation on Early's part, exhaustion and hunger among the Southern troops that led them to fall out of ranks to pillage Union camps, and Sheridan's rallying of his soldiers combined to bring the third ignominious defeat in a month to the Army of the Valley. Cedar Creek essentially ended major military activity in the Valley. Lincoln offered Sheridan "the thanks of the Nation, and my own personal admiration and gratitude, for the month's operations in the Shenandoah Valley; and especially for the splendid work of October 19, 1864." Lee recalled most of Early's men to the Army of Northern Virginia before the end of the year, leaving a skeleton command under Old Jube to play out a few final scenes that winter and in early spring 1865. The Federals followed suit, with Sheridan returning to Grant in time to earn additional fame during the Appomattox campaign.

Though less fabled than the 1862 Valley campaign, operations in the Shenandoah between May and October 1864 wielded considerably greater influence on the course of the war. Never again would the Confederacy draw sustenance from the region's rich farmland, a logistical disaster rivaling the loss of huge portions of Tennessee during the first half of 1862 and Sherman's gutting of central Georgia during the "March to the Sea." Strategically the South lost access to a vital position on the western flank of Washington and Baltimore. Henceforth no Southern army would tramp the Valley Pike en route to a raid across the Potomac. Together with the captures of Mobile Bay and Atlanta, Sheridan's victories ensured Republican success in November 1864. That verdict at the polls, in turn, extinguished any chance that the North might stop short of a complete victory based on restoration of the Union and the destruction of slavery. Finally, Sheridan's methodical burning constituted the first large-scale demonstration that the strategy of exhaustion could accomplish the psychological and logistical damage envisioned by Grant.

The scale of the 1864 campaign also dwarfed that of Jackson's in 1862. The armies marched hundreds of miles farther (about 1,500 as against 650 on the Southern side by Jedediah Hotchkiss's reckoning), fought harder, and, in the case of the Confederates, endured far greater privation. In the six largest battles during 1862 (Kernstown, McDowell, Front Royal, Winchester, Cross Keys, and Port Republic), total casualties were about 5,500 for the North, half of which were prisoners, and 2,750 for the South—very light losses when measured against even middling Civil War actions. Of these six, only First Winchester really deserves to be called a battle; the rest merely amounted to large skirmishes in which each side usually lost a few hundred men. In contrast, the six bloodiest battles in 1864—Lynchburg, the Monocacy, Second Kernstown, Third Winchester, Fisher's Hill, and Cedar Creek—resulted in more than fifteen thousand Union and nearly ten thousand Confederate casualties. At both Third Winchester and Cedar Creek, Sheridan lost as many men as all of Jackson's opponents combined during the entire 1862 Valley campaign.

Jubal Early is usually the big loser in comparative estimates of the two campaigns. Both contemporary and later critics used Jackson's performance as an ideal against which to judge Early. Jackson's campaign *was* a classic example of clever maneuvering, but Early's efforts hold up very well against that lofty standard. The quality of Northern leadership favored Jackson to a striking degree. Banks and Frémont demonstrated nothing but utter incompetence, and the absence of an overall Federal commander prevented adequate coordination of efforts against Jackson. Early thrashed the minimally gifted Hunter and Wallace, but Sheridan possessed the talent, numbers, and broad authority to wage a savagely effective campaign of attrition and exhaustion. In his entire Confederate career, Jackson never confronted a man of Sheridan's ability. Moreover, though writers frequently claim that Jackson defeated forty to sixty thousand Federals, Union forces in the Valley in 1862 seldom counted even twenty thousand bayonets, and those men often lacked high morale and adequate supplies. With about fifteen thousand men, Early fought a veteran army of thirty-five to forty thousand led by the aggressive Sheridan. Unlike Jackson, Early had absolutely no hope of gaining numerical superiority over the enemy through maneuver.

In sum, Jackson enjoyed advantages that made his task in 1862 much easier than Early's in 1864. Against weak opponents leading second-line troops, Jackson won a series of small victories that enabled him to accomplish his goals. Against equally weak leadership during June and July 1864, Early also won victories and accomplished his goals. He then failed against the powerful and confident Sheridan. Strategically, Jackson prevented McDowell and Banks from reinforcing McClellan below Richmond, while Early occupied more than forty thousand soldiers and one of Grant's best generals for several months. Two natural questions arise in any comparison of the two campaigns. First, could Early have matched Jackson's dazzling success in 1862? Probably not, though almost certainly he would have emerged triumphant. Second, would Jackson's presence in September and October 1864 have stymied Sheridan's designs? Again, probably not. The progress of the campaign undoubtedly would have been different, but not the outcome. Sheridan's gifts as a commander and the Federal force's superiority in numbers would have overcome the best efforts of any general laboring under the handicaps placed on Jubal Early.

Despite their decisive character, operations in the Valley during 1864 will most likely never inspire the mixture of uncritical adulation and intense interest like that directed toward Jackson's Valley campaign. The reasons are understandable. Neither Sheridan nor Early can match the weirdly brilliant Jackson as a romantic, arresting figure. The former's squat stature, mean-spirited nature, and relentless destruction of the verdant Valley disqualify him; similarly, an acid tongue, abject defeat, and self-serving postwar writings limit enthusiasm for Early. Jackson's martyrdom enhances his mythical standing, thus widening the gap between him and the others. A successful campaign against the odds such as Jackson waged also generates more admiration than Sheridan's praiseworthy utilization of overpowering strength or Early's daring but disastrous effort. Finally, chronology works against 1864. Many people prefer to study the campaigns of 1862, when the South stood a chance of victory and gallantry seemed still to be a part of war, rather than examine the grinding brutality and apparently senseless slaughter of 1864.

This relative neglect of the 1864 campaigning in the Valley slights one of the most fascinating and important episodes in Civil War history. The military and political stakes were immense. War on civilians first debuted on a theater-wide scale, and tactical operations ran the gamut from guerrilla activity to the grand encounter at Cedar Creek. Without an appreciation of why the Shenandoah Valley became first a battleground and then a wasteland, it is impossible to understand fully the last year of the war.

Jubal A. Early
and Confederate Leadership

JEFFRY D. WERT

In the span of a month—from September 19 to October 19, 1864—Confederate Lieutenant General Jubal Anderson Early suffered a string of battlefield defeats unmatched by any other army commander in the Civil War. During those thirty days, the Union Army of the Shenandoah under the command of Major General Philip H. Sheridan won victories at Third Winchester, Fisher's Hill, Tom's Brook, and Cedar Creek and applied the torch to a large swath of the Shenandoah Valley. By the campaign's conclusion, Early's army was crippled as a fighting force, and the granary of the Confederacy lay in ruins.

History, in turn, favors neither the fool nor the loser. It possesses a harshness; and in the case of Jubal Early, history's judgment has been severe. Flaws within the man's character and his generalship contributed to the outcome of the final struggle for the Valley of Virginia. But Early was an officer burdened with a bold strategy imposed by Robert E. Lee, a numerically inferior command, and the long shadow of Thomas J. "Stonewall" Jackson. When the Confederate cause required a flawless performance in the Shenandoah Valley, Early came up short.

Early had been in command of the Confederate Second Corps less than three weeks when Lee summoned him to army headquarters outside of Cold Harbor, Virginia, on June 12, 1864. The pair met in private. Lee told Early to take his three infantry divisions and two artillery battalions as rapidly as possible to the Shenandoah Valley, where Union Major General David Hunter's twenty thousand–man force was approaching the vital Southern rail hub at Lynchburg. Early should attack Hunter, and, if circumstances permitted, proceed northward down the Valley, cross into Maryland—gathering supplies en route—and threaten Washington, D.C. and Baltimore.

Lee viewed the proposed operation as a gamble. While Hunter's threat to Lynchburg had to be eliminated, Lee hoped also to regain the strategic initiative in the Old Dominion. With his army locked in place outside Richmond by George G. Meade's Army of the Potomac (under the direction of General-in-Chief Ulysses S. Grant), Lee saw in Early's operation an opportunity to break the stalemate. He believed that such a strike across the Potomac River would compel Grant to detach units from Meade's army and thereby provide an opening to launch an offensive against the weakened Federals. It was a refashioning of the strategy of two years earlier when Jackson stormed through the Valley, disrupting Federal operations east and west of the Blue Ridge.

Lee's plan must have brightened the dark eyes of the ambitious Early, for only Jackson and James Longstreet had been given such responsibility by Lee in the past. Once undertaken, however, the audacious enterprise gained a momentum of its own, and the stakes grew higher for both Lee and Grant. Early took with him a fourth of the army's infantry. For Lee to relinquish such manpower, the results had to justify the costs. Early, indeed, carried with him a heavy responsibility. When he walked out of Lee's headquarters, the war in Virginia took a new direction for the summer and fall of 1864.

During the next six weeks, Early fulfilled Lee's expectations and goals. His corps—Jackson's renowned foot cavalry—relieved Lynchburg by chasing Hunter into the Alleghenies, raced down the Shenandoah Valley into Maryland, defeated a patchwork Union force at Monocacy, and, in Early's terse words to a staff officer, "scared Abe Lincoln like h[ell]" before the gates of Washington. When forced to retire to Virginia, Early did so with skill and swiftness, punishing his pursuers at Cool Spring on July 18. Six days later his command routed a Union force at the Battle of Second Kernstown, and on July 30 his cavalry burned Chambersburg, Pennsylvania. Lee could only be satisfied with the achievements, as Grant forwarded the Sixth Corps and detoured two divisions of the Nineteenth Corps to the endangered capital.

By the end of the first week in August, Early's Army of the Valley rested in the lower Shenandoah north of Winchester. Beyond the Confederate camp around Harpers Ferry, the Union Army of the Shenandoah was forming under Philip H. Sheridan's command. Early's successful raid and its aftermath had brought a major response from Grant, and the Federal commander had created a weapon, in size and in prowess, unlike any previous Northern force assigned to the Valley. The debits and credits of Early as a man and as a general now counted for much.

Lee well knew that Early could be a difficult individual with whom to work. The commanding general even chided the corps commander for some of his habits by calling Early "my bad old man." Early was irascible, opinionated, and cynical—a man who detested pretentiousness. A fault-finder by nature, he had made numerous enemies among the officers of the army. He could be brutally honest and deprecating when he witnessed the failures of others; he could be almost blind when the mistakes were of his own making, bristling at criticism leveled against him.

Early had other deficiencies of personality and leadership as an army commander, but perhaps none was more important than his relationship with ranking subordinates. With him in the Valley were four of the finest combat officers in Lee's army—Major Generals John C. Breckinridge, Robert E. Rodes, John B. Gordon, and Stephen Dodson Ramseur. Early possessed an indisposition to confer with or to act upon the advice of these experienced, capable lieutenants. Assigning to Breckinridge an unofficial demi-corps composed of the divisions of Gordon and Gabriel C. Wharton, Early neither confided in Breckinridge nor used his talents to the fullest. The darker aspects of Early's character came forth against officers he viewed as rivals, a phenomenon best illustrated by his relationship with Gordon. A superb officer, Gordon was a rising star whose performances on several battlefields marked him for greater responsibility. But Early disliked the Georgian, probably resenting the praise given to him; Gordon, in turn, cared little for the carping, critical Early, and their relationship worsened throughout the campaign.

Major General John Brown Gordon

Early did enjoy the respect and affection of the soldiers in the ranks. The men, said one of them, had "a great fondness" for "Old Jube" or "Old Jubilee," as they called him. His eccentricities and lack of sentimentality appealed to them. He and they were kindred spirits. Whenever he rode along a column of marchers, the men cheered and laughed. But after he passed, "some wag would shout after him one or another of the old army gags of those days. He would wheel his horse to see who had insulted him, but nobody knew, and he had no means of finding out."

Old Jube possessed neither charisma nor an imposing physical presence. Rheumatism had bent his spine, and the stoop-shouldered general on horseback looked, wrote a Confederate, "as preternaturally solemn as a country coroner going to his first inquest." Early's full gray beard and dark eyes reminded another of "a very malignant and very hairy spider." He was simply, stated a third Rebel, "a queer fish."

If Early lacked the appearance of a warrior, he had a warrior's soul. His valor in combat was unquestioned. "He was always ready for a fight," asserted one of his veterans, "and was never happier than when in a battle." Captain Samuel Buck of the 13th Virginia, writing years later, agreed: "I had seen him at times and places that tried men's souls, and he was always in the thickest of the battle." Gordon even admitted in his memoirs that Early was "one of the coolest and most imperturbable of men under fire and in extremity." But Gordon cautioned that Early lacked "the courage of one's convictions. . . . He strikes in the dark, madly, wildly, and often impotently."

By training, by experience, by temperament, Early was an infantryman. As such, he had prejudice toward and a misunderstanding of the mounted arm. For him, as commander of an army, that viewpoint and lack of knowledge affected his leadership. During the winter of 1863–64, while in charge of the Valley District, Early developed a strong dislike for the ill-disciplined cavalry units he directed and carried that bias with him into the forthcoming campaign. His prejudice toward the cavalry was compounded by the inferior quality of the mounted forces in the Valley army. The cavalry regiments were crippled by a lack of discipline, insufficient and ineffective arms, and a shortage of horseflesh. Their prowess in combat had eroded as the conflict wore on, and Early neither liked nor had confidence in most of the mounted commanders. The inferior quality of Early's cavalry became a serious handicap during the campaign.

No single factor affected Early's generalship in the struggle for the Valley more than the disparity in numbers between the two opposing armies. By the first week in August, Early counted roughly nine thousand effectives in four infantry divisions, eight hundred artillerymen, and just more than four thousand cavalrymen, for a total of approximately fourteen thousand. Lee augmented Early's strength in mid-August with Joseph B. Kershaw's infantry division, Fitzhugh Lee's cavalry division, and an artillery battalion, bringing the Confederate total to over nineteen thousand men. Just before Third Winchester, however, Kershaw's command and the artillery battalion started back to rejoin Lee's army, thereby missing that engagement and Fisher's Hill. In the crucial month between Third Winchester and Cedar Creek, Early never commanded more than sixteen thousand men. Sheridan, by contrast, directed a powerful weapon. The Union Army of the Shenandoah Valley had nearly thirty-five thousand infantry and artillery effectives and eight thousand cavalry. The Military District of Harpers Ferry added another five thousand troops, giving Sheridan a numerical edge of roughly three to one over his opponent. Against such a host, the Confederates could afford few mistakes.

The duel between Early and Sheridan began on August 10, when the Federals marched southward against the Rebels. Early retired to Fisher's Hill, where the opponents tested each other for a few days. When Kershaw and Fitz Lee arrived at Front Royal on Sheridan's flank, the Northerners withdrew to the Harpers Ferry–Halltown area. From August 22 until September 18, operations embraced a rough triangle from Winchester to Berryville to Harpers Ferry in the lower Valley.

During these weeks, which a Federal described as "mimic war," Early ably fulfilled Lee's orders to threaten Maryland and Pennsylvania and to close the Baltimore & Ohio Railroad and the Chesapeake and Ohio Canal. He accomplished this, in his

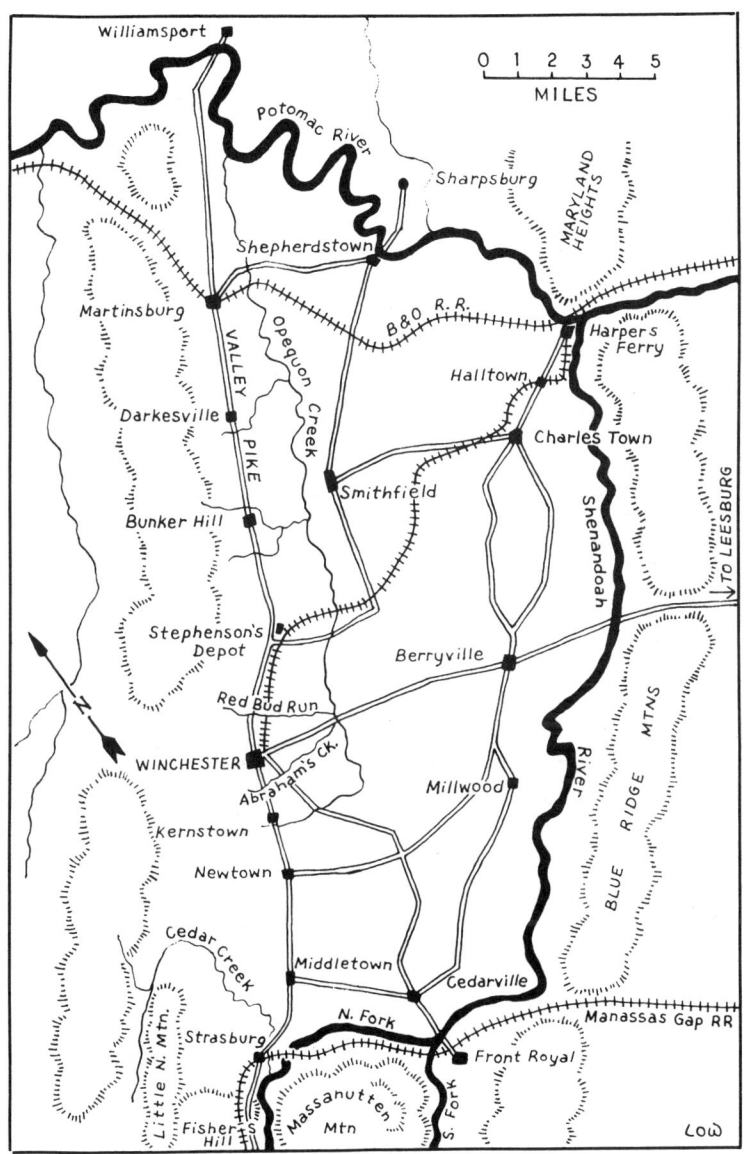

The Lower Shenandoah Valley

own words, by using "my forces so as to display them at different points with great rapidity, and thereby keep up the impression that they were much larger than they really were." It was a pattern of march-countermarch that took a physical toll from the Southern infantry. Major Henry Kyd Douglas, a staff officer, called it "a reckless game under his [Sheridan's] nose." But given Lee's strategy, Early had little recourse.

Early, however, came to the belief that Sheridan "possessed an excessive caution which amounted to timidity." The Confederate commander made this critical misjudgment because he could not understand why his Union counterpart huddled his army behind fieldworks. Early did not know that, while en route from Petersburg to Harpers Ferry, Sheridan had stopped in Washington. There Chief-of-Staff Henry W. Halleck or Secretary of War Edwin M. Stanton, or both, warned him of the political consequences for Lincoln's reelection of another battlefield defeat in the Shenandoah Valley. The pair of Union officials enjoined Sheridan to act with caution, and he complied until Grant personally ordered the advance that resulted in Third Winchester.

Early's assessment of Sheridan's generalship and his mistrust of Southern cavalry combined on September 18 to imperil the Valley army and shape the tactical pattern of Third Winchester. Early learned on the seventeenth that railroad repair crews were at work on the tracks of the Baltimore & Ohio at Martinsburg. Instead of sending a cavalry force to ascertain the accuracy of the report, Early dispatched the infantry divisions of Gordon and Rodes and a cavalry brigade. The Confederates started that afternoon, arriving at Martinsburg the next morning. Early, who accompanied the detachment, found no work crews but learned that Grant had recently visited with Sheridan. Accurately assessing the portent of Grant's presence in the region, Early raced his divisions back toward Winchester. By nightfall Rodes's and Gordon's men were encamped between Bunker Hill and Stephenson's Depot. Wharton's division lay at Winchester; Ramseur's lay east of the town guarding the road to Berryville, where Sheridan's army was located.

Early's "wild goose chase" on September 18, as one South-erner called it, forced him to give battle at Winchester the next day when Sheridan advanced. His army faced piecemeal de-struction if the Federals overwhelmed Ramseur and swept into Winchester. Because he believed Sheridan to be an excessively cautious foe, Early had returned Kershaw's division and an ar-tillery battalion to Lee on the fifteenth and sent half his infan-try on a mission designed for cavalry. By nightfall of the eighteenth, wrote a Confederate brigade commander, "Early had his troops stretched out and separated like a string of glass beads with a knot between each one."

Before daylight on September 19, the Yankees moved against Early's "string of glass beads." Blue-jacketed cavalry, brushing aside Ramseur's picket force, surged through the Berryville Canyon, a two-mile-long defile east of Winchester, and opened the path for the Union infantry and artillery. Ramseur's foot soldiers opposed the advance but faced annihilation before Early could regroup. The Confederates needed time, and Sheridan gave it to them when he blundered grievously by or-dering twenty thousand infantrymen and dozens of guns through the canyon. Massive delays in the crowded canyon de-layed Union infantry attacks until 11:40 A.M., by which time Early had his divisions and batteries in place.

Once the armies locked in combat, Early performed with tactical skill and daring. While Fisher's Hill should have been his place in battle, Early utilized the terrain at Winchester as well as could be expected. When the morning's Union as-sault rolled forward, the Confederates fought valiantly, and Early unleashed a vicious counterattack into a gap in the Union lines created by Sheridan's faulty tactical arrangement. The counterassault by Rodes's division into the center of the Federal line nearly inflicted a stunning defeat upon the Yankees. Sheridan stopped it with his last division on the field, but the Rebels had come close. When Sheridan thrusted, Early parried and then counterthrusted. By one o'clock in the after-noon, the field still belonged to the Southerners.

Early probably could have extricated his outnumbered units with little loss, but that would have meant relinquishing a

Major General Stephen Dodson Ramseur

stoutly defended field. Perhaps Early should have withdrawn, but he chose to stand. He retrenched his lines closer to Winchester, shifted units to counter the Federal cavalry north

Major General Robert Emmett Rodes

of town, and awaited the renewal of the battle between the infantry. When the two divisions of George Crook's Eighth
Corps opened the final Union assault at roughly three o'clock,

the Confederates held for more than two hours. A floodtide of Yankee manpower, beginning with a lightning strike by Sheridan's horsemen, finally engulfed the exhausted defenders. Only the discipline and experience of some of Early's infantry and artillery spared him from a possible rout.

Early suggested to Lee that his mounted units caused the defeat: "The enemy's very great superiority in cavalry and the comparative inefficiency of ours turned the scale against us." The Confederate horsemen had not fought particularly well, but they, like their comrades in the infantry and artillery, were overwhelmed by Federal numerical superiority. A Northerner, witnessing the final assault, likened the rank upon rank of Union soldiers to "foaming waves of ocean" that cascaded over the beleaguered defenders. Those waves determined the outcome of Third Winchester. What Early neglected to tell Lee was that faulty prebattle dispositions invited the defeat.

The Confederate Army of the Valley retired to Fisher's Hill during the night of September 19–20. This was "the only place where a stand could be made," Early informed Lee, with any "hope of arresting Sheridan's progress." It should have been Early's chosen ground in the first place; now circumstances dictated its selection. Writing in his memoirs, Early explained more fully why he stopped at the eminence south of Strasburg. "To have retired beyond this point," he argued, "would have rendered it necessary for me to fall back to some of the gaps of the Blue Ridge, at the upper part of the Valley, and I determined therefore to make a show of a stand here, with the hopes that the enemy would be deterred from attacking me in this position, as had been the case in August."

What was true in August, however, no longer held. The Yankees and their commander, flush from the victory at Third Winchester, were willing to test the Confederate works on Fisher's Hill, which a Federal soldier described "as the bugbear of the valley." The rock-strewn bluff, wedged between Massanutten Mountain to the east and Little North Mountain to the west, was a nearly impregnable position if adequately defended. But Third Winchester had cost Early approximately 30 percent of his army, and the four-mile front exceeded the limits of Early's thinned ranks. The Confederate position, wrote a Union officer, was "too big for his [Early's] enfeebled army." The faulty disposition of his units, as well as a lack of numbers, compromised Early's decision to defend Fisher's Hill. The vulnerable key to the position was at the western end of the line where the bluff leveled out into low ground at the foot of Little North Mountain. Here Early placed the troublesome cavalry against which he had railed for two months and to which he attributed his defeat at Winchester. It was a grievous tactical blunder, inexplicable given Early's ability and experience.

When the Union attack came at Fisher's Hill on September 22, Crook's Yankees poured down Little North Mountain into the flank of Major General Lunsford L. Lomax's Southern horsemen. The Rebel mounted units disintegrated before the onslaught, placing Early's entire front in danger. The Confederate commander had planned a withdrawal for that night, but it was too late. Having disregarded the absence of Crook's two divisions, Early was surprised by the flanking attack. Sheridan, in turn, committed his other infantry commands, and the Confederate line collapsed. The retreat from the field quickly turned into a stampede that continued for miles.

Once again, Early held the cavalry responsible for the rout. The mounted command, he asserted to Lee three days later, "has been the source of all my disasters." Again, too, Early was blind to his own culpability. He knew the shortcomings of the cavalry, did nothing to rectify the problems, and then placed the horsemen along the weakest sector of his line. John Gordon argued correctly in his reminiscences that it "is not just to blame the troops. There are conditions in war when courage, firmness, steadiness of nerve, and self-reliance are of small avail. Such were the conditions at Fisher's Hill." Sheridan simply outgeneraled Early on September 22.

Third Winchester and Fisher's Hill opened the upper Shenandoah Valley to the Union army. While the Confederates retreated to the western foot of the Blue Ridge at Brown's Gap, the Federals marched to Harrisonburg in the heart of the region. For the next two weeks the opponents remained in these

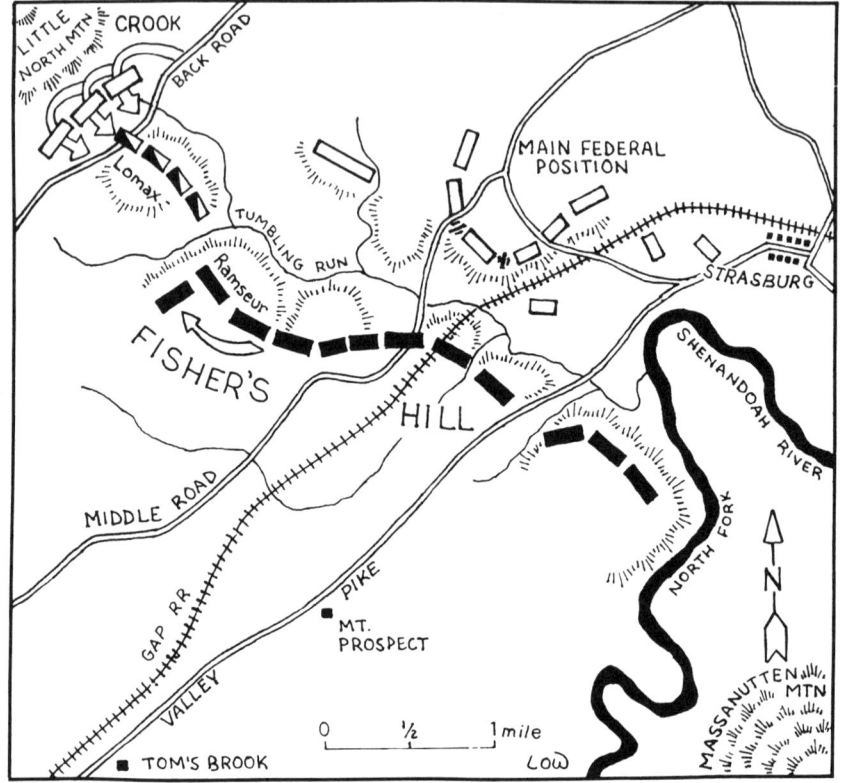

Battle of Fisher's Hill, September 22, 1864

general areas. Lee returned Kershaw's division and the artillery battalion to Early and added the cavalry brigade of Thomas L. Rosser. The Yankees, meanwhile, roamed through the countryside burning mills, barns, and crops and gathering livestock. Sheridan, Grant, Halleck, and Stanton exchanged a series of telegrams on the future course of Union strategy before Sheridan began a retrograde movement northward on October 6. For the next three days Sheridan's cavalry implemented what Valley residents called "The Burning." By the tenth, the Federal units were filing into camps south of Middletown along Cedar Creek.

Early did little to prevent these days of fire and smoke. His cavalry, even with the addition of Rosser's brigade, could not stop the Federal troopers. When Sheridan began the withdrawal, Early sent his mounted units in pursuit and trailed with the infantry and artillery. Skirmishes between horsemen ignited and flared for three days. Finally, on October 9, Sheridan unleashed his cavalry against Early's at Tom's Brook, which resulted in a Confederate rout and a twenty-mile flight dubbed the "Woodstock Races." Early has to share with Rosser the censure for this ignominious defeat because he allowed his outnumbered cavalrymen to be far in advance of infantry support.

The Army of the Valley reached Strasburg on October 13. A few miles to the north, beyond Cedar Creek, was the Army of the Shenandoah. As Early explained it later, "I was now compelled to move back for want of provisions and forage, or attack the enemy in his position with the hope of driving him from it, and I determined to attack." Early's decision to assume the offensive was bolstered by an October 12 letter from Lee. Lee had watched the tide of defeat in the Valley, reinforced Early, and defended his subordinate against a storm of criticism. The entire Confederate campaign had been predicated upon boldness, a gamble that might stay the darkness that was descending upon the Confederacy. Lee and the cause required victory in the Shenandoah Valley, and the commanding general reminded Early that "I have weakened myself very much to strengthen you. It was done with the expectation of enabling you to gain such success you could return the troops if not rejoin me yourself." Lee offered suggestions, then added that "you had better move against him and endeavor to crush him." Early could achieve a victory, believed Lee, with a coordinated attack utilizing all of the Confederate units. "I do not think," concluded Lee, "Sheridan's infantry or cavalry numerically as large as you suppose."

Lee's assessment of the strength of Sheridan's army had guided his strategy in the Valley since August. While Early forwarded accurate evaluations of his opponent's numbers, Lee dismissed them as excessive. Lee, in turn, prodded Early into action, burdening him with an audacious, risky strategy against a formidable enemy. At no other time in the war had the brilliant Lee so miscalculated the strength of any enemy force.

Early thus undertook the offensive at Cedar Creek because Lee expected it and because the only alternative was to retire for want of supplies. Then, contrary to his usual method of decision making, he utilized the talents of his subordinates. On October 17, Early sent Gordon, Brigadier General Clement A. Evans, and Jedediah Hotchkiss, a topographical engineer, to survey Federal dispositions from Massanutten Mountain. The next day Early convened a council of war, and the three officers proposed a night march by the Second Corps to a point beyond Sheridan's left flank preparatory to an assault by the entire army at first light on the nineteenth. Division commander John Pegram voiced strong objections to the plan, but Early approved the scheme.

The Second Corps, with Gordon commanding, started its march at 8:00 P.M. on October 18. Jackson's old foot cavalry forded the North Fork of the Shenandoah River near Fisher's Hill, followed a "pig's path" along the base of the Massanutten, and crossed the river a second time. The other units, meanwhile, moved into their positions, and well before daylight on the nineteenth the Confederates were poised to strike. It was an achievement unparalleled in the Civil War. Early and Gordon should share the credit for flawless execution of a difficult operation.

The Second Corps and Kershaw's division, shielded by a heavy fog, stormed into the Union camps and works at approximately 5:40 A.M. During the next three hours the gray-coated infantrymen routed Crook's command, two divisions of the Nineteenth Corps, and J. Howard Kitching's Provisional Division and drove two divisions of the Sixth Corps into retreat. The Southern offensive, in the opinion of a Federal officer, was "as brilliant a feat of arms as the war afforded."

Jubal Early rode onto the Cedar Creek battlefield before 7:30 A.M. Behind him on the Valley Pike came Gabriel Wharton's

Battle of Cedar Creek—Confederate Attack on the Camps of the Federal Sixth Corps

infantry division and batteries of artillery. Early soon met Gordon, and the Georgian summarized the situation while Old Jube strained to get his bearings in the fog. When Gordon departed to direct the Second Corps' and Kershaw's assaults against two divisions of the Sixth Corps, Early spurred northward to the southern outskirts of Middletown, where he conferred with Dodson Ramseur and John Pegram. The two division leaders requested support for an attack on George Getty's division of the Sixth Corps deployed in Middletown's cemetery at the southwestern edge of the town. Their commands had been repulsed, and Ramseur and Pegram asked that Wharton's division be brought into action. "I ordered Wharton's division forward at once," Early wrote afterward, "and directed Generals Ramseur and Pegram to put it where it was required." Early had acted hastily, and in doing so made a crucial mistake. Wharton's initial orders were to "press up the pike." If Early meant for Wharton to pass through Middletown, he erred badly when he committed the division to an attack on Getty. The Valley Pike was the key to the Southern victory: if the Confederates had cleared Middletown before the Union cavalry were posted north of the town along the Pike, the entire Federal army could have been outflanked, as the Yankees would not have been able to regroup and most likely would have had to retreat to Winchester. A Union captain justifiably termed Early's decision "his fatal error."

Wharton's men, like Ramseur's and Pegram's before them, ran head-on into a wall of musketry and retired. At 9:30 A.M., the Federals abandoned the cemetery as Gordon's troops, having driven back the other two divisions of the Sixth Corps, were closing on the right and rear of the cemetery. Within the next hour, the Union corps retreated to a new line north of the village and Gordon found Early. The ensuing conversation, as related by Gordon in his reminiscences, has formed the cornerstone of the case against Early at Cedar Creek. "Well, Gordon, this is glory enough for one day," Early stated when the two officers met. "This is the 19th. Precisely one month ago to-day we were going in the opposite direction."

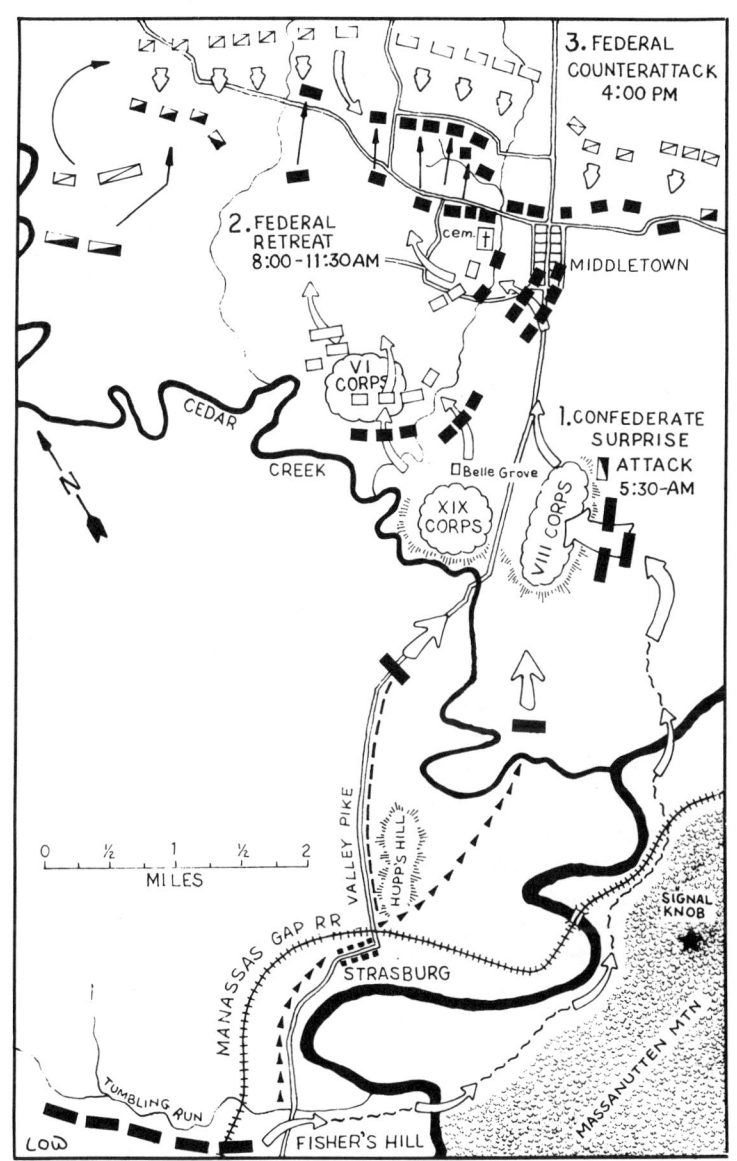

3. FEDERAL COUNTERATTACK 4:00 PM

2. FEDERAL RETREAT 8:00-11:30 AM

cem.

MIDDLETOWN

CEDAR

CREEK

VI CORPS

□ Belle Grove

XIX CORPS

VIII CORPS

1. CONFEDERATE SURPRISE ATTACK 5:30-AM

N

0   ½   1   ½   2
MILES

VALLEY PIKE

HUPP'S HILL

MANASSAS GAP RR

SIGNAL KNOB

STRASBURG

TUMBLING RUN

LOW

FISHER'S HILL

MASSANUTTEN MTN

Battle of Cedar Creek, October 19, 1864

"It is very well so far, general," Gordon replied, "but we have one more blow to strike, and then there will not be left an organized company of infantry in Sheridan's army." Pointing at the fleeing Sixth Corps, Gordon added that he had ordered another advance upon the Northerners.

"No use in that; they will all go directly," Early responded.

"That is the Sixth Corps, general," replied Gordon. "It will not go unless we drive it from the field."

"Yes, it will go too, directly," said Early.

"My heart went into my boots," Gordon recalled in describing his reaction to Early's final words. "Visions of the fatal halt on the first day at Gettysburg, and of the whole day's hesitation to permit an assault on Grant's exposed flank on the 6th of May in the Wilderness, rose before me. And so it came to pass that the fatal halting, the hesitation, the spasmodic firing, and the isolated movements in the face of the sullen, slow, and orderly retreat of this superb Federal corps, lost us the great opportunity, and converted the brilliant victory of the morning into disastrous defeat in the evening."

It was a damaging indictment by Gordon, and one accepted by historians. The facts of the tactical situation, however, favor a different interpretation. The Confederate assault had crested just beyond Middletown, where seventy-five hundred Union cavalrymen held the ground east of the Pike. The divisions of Pegram and Wharton had encountered this barrier and had stopped. Ramseur was closing on Pegram's left, but neither Kershaw nor Evans had brought his troops into line when this alleged conversation transpired. The Rebels were bone weary; hundreds were trailing behind after plundering the Union camps. If Early had directed the assault envisioned by Gordon, it could not have begun much before 11:30 or noon. By then the Union infantry had re-formed along the cavalry's line, and Sheridan was on the field.

Early did not lose the Battle of Cedar Creek because of a "fatal delay," as Douglas Southall Freeman called it. The masterful offensive of the morning had reached temporary limits. The tactical initiative shifted to the Federals once their horsemen secured the Valley Pike. The Confederate commander's critical error occurred earlier when he redirected Wharton against Getty's troops. Early also had detached Lunsford L. Lomax's cavalry division on an ill-defined mission toward Front Royal, keeping only a small brigade of cavalry with the army. Had he retained Lomax, the Southern cavalrymen could have seized the roadway and delayed, if not prevented, the Federals from controlling the Pike. Neither Early nor other ranking officers, even years later, saw the Valley Pike for what it was—the avenue of victory.

At this stage in the battle—at roughly midday—the Confederates paused, holding a three-mile line from the Pike westward. "I determined, therefore," Early reported, "to content myself with trying to hold the advantages I had gained until all my troops had come up and the captured property was secured." Daring gave way to caution; Early seemed content with the victory that had been achieved. At 1:00 P.M. he sent forward the divisions of Evans, Kershaw, and Ramseur in a reconnaissance-in-force. They advanced a mile and a half, weakly probed the Union line, and halted. Early apparently dismissed the possibility of a Federal counterattack and, instead of pulling back the three divisions, left them in an exposed position with both flanks vulnerable. It was a tactical blunder comparable to the faulty deployment at Fisher's Hill.

At 4:00 P.M. Sheridan launched his army at the three Southern divisions, and the Rebel line dissolved under the onslaught. When Federal cavalry caved in the Confederate left flank, even veteran soldiers panicked. Except for some isolated pockets of resistance, the Army of the Valley fled in a rout. All that had been won in the morning and more was lost in a matter of one or two hours. Cedar Creek became a bitter defeat for the Confederates.

The battle of October 19 virtually finished the duel between Early and Sheridan. The invincibility of Southern arms in the Shenandoah Valley had been broken for good. At Cedar Creek, as at Winchester and Fisher's Hill, Southern soldiers fought valiantly, but circumstances and a handful of critical errors doomed the Rebels. Early subsequently addressed the question of why he attacked at Cedar Creek: "It may be asked why with my small force I made the attack. I can only say we had been fighting large odds during the whole war, and I knew there was no chance of lessening them. It was of the utmost consequence that Sheridan should be prevented from sending troops to Grant, and General Lee, in a letter received a day or two before, had expressed an earnest desire that a victory should be gained in the valley if possible, and it could not be gained without fighting for it."

So Early risked the fight against long odds. The entire campaign had been predicated upon such a strategy. In the end, however, those odds mattered above all else. The Federals fought well, even brilliantly at times, and with their numerical superiority decisively defeated the Rebels. Sheridan could afford tactical mistakes; Early could not. For Jubal Early, the outcome overshadowed all else. Then and thereafter he was unjustly compared to Stonewall Jackson: where Old Jack had brought victory Old Jube brought defeat and ruin. But Early had fulfilled much of Lee's gambling strategy. He forced Grant to detach troops from Meade's army and kept that opponent at bay for weeks; when the battle was joined, his army inflicted roughly twelve thousand casualties while incurring fewer than ten thousand.

Still, Early and his army ultimately failed. He was a flawed man and general, and such failings were magnified in the crucible of the campaign. Perhaps a fair judgment of Early could be left to two men in the ranks—a Southerner and a Northerner. "I think," concluded a Confederate private, "General Early did everything a commander could do in the Valley with the number of men he had in his command." The Yankee, writing four days after Cedar Creek, observed, "Poor Early! The fates seem against him."

Union Generalship
in the 1864 Valley Campaign

A. WILSON GREENE

On July 12, 1864, Assistant Secretary of War Charles Anderson Dana painted a grim picture of the Federal military situation around Washington: "Nothing can possibly be done here toward pursuing or cutting off the enemy for want of a commander," he informed the general-in-chief. "There is no head to the whole, and it seems indispensable that you should at once appoint one. . . . General Halleck will not give orders, except as he receives them, the President will give none; and until you direct positively and explicitly what is to be done everything will go on in the deplorable and fatal way in which it has gone for the past week." Slow at first to appreciate the importance of the Shenandoah Valley in his grand strategy for winning the war, Lieutenant General Ulysses S. Grant recognized Jubal A. Early's campaign to the outskirts of Washington as a serious threat to the success of his comprehensive program. Grant agreed with Dana that the first step toward neutralizing that threat would be to rectify the tangled administrative situation prevailing along the Potomac.

Four independent army entities operated within fifty miles of the capital, all looking to the War Department for guidance. Like so many country sheriffs confined to their tiny jurisdictions, the commanders of the Middle, West Virginia, Susquehanna, and Washington departments lacked the necessary authority and coordination to cope with an active and mobile adversary. Grant's decision to bivouac with the Army of the Potomac confined him to the steaming trenches around Petersburg, leaving only Chief-of-Staff Henry W. Halleck in a position to harmonize the efforts of the various armies. "Old Brains," however, possessed neither the ability nor the initiative to discharge such a weighty responsibility. Halleck served merely as a communications link among the War Department, Grant, and the lieutenant general's seventeen immediate subordinates.

Clearly, Grant needed one man to direct operations against Early, a requirement rendered more urgent by a Confederate victory at Kernstown, Virginia, on July 24. The administration, however, vetoed Grant's first choice, Major General William B. Franklin, a former engineer exiled to the Trans-Mississippi after fumbling at Fredericksburg in 1862. "I do not insist ... upon General Franklin," Grant told Lincoln. "All I ask is that one general officer, in whom I and yourself have confidence, should command the whole." The general-in-chief next advanced the name of Major General George G. Meade, temperamental commander of the Army of the Potomac. "With General Meade in command," Grant wrote, "I would have every confidence that all the troops ... would be used to the very best advantage." Meade's removal would also relieve Grant of a festering personality problem between "the old snapping turtle" and his corps commanders; but Lincoln vetoed this idea, too. The president feared that the public would view such a transfer as a demotion for the victor of Gettysburg. Lincoln then requested a meeting with Grant at Fort Monroe to review other options. Little is known about this historic conference of July 31, but on the following day Grant announced that the thirty-three-year-old head of Meade's cavalry, Major General Philip H. Sheridan, would assume tactical command of a new administrative establishment christened the Middle Military Division.

Lincoln and Halleck greeted the appointment with reservations, while Secretary of War Edwin M. Stanton openly opposed Sheridan as too young and inexperienced. The president reluctantly approved the arrangement, but only on a temporary basis. Moreover, Major General David Hunter, Sheridan's senior, would remain in overall charge of the division entrusting Sheridan with operations in the field. The general-in-chief journeyed to Frederick, Maryland, on August 5, to confer with Hunter and convey his objectives for the campaign. When Hunter learned that Sheridan would actually lead the troops, he correctly grasped Grant's lack of confidence in him. Hunter asked to be relieved, a request that met with quick acceptance. Free now of any encumbrances in his new post, Sheridan made his way north to assume command.

Sheridan owed his elevation solely to Grant. The young cavalry officer had not lobbied personally for his new position and obviously brought no particular political clout to the job. The disaster at the Crater on July 30, however, persuaded Grant not only that the capture of Petersburg would be a lengthy endeavor, but also that a large force of cavalry would not be required in the operation. Hence, Sheridan was available. Major General William T. Sherman praised Grant upon the selection of his old comrade: "I am glad you have given Sheridan the command of the forces to defend Washington. He will worry Early to death." The common soldiers, however, viewed their new general with a mixture of "surprise and disappointment." They, and the president, would carefully assess Grant's judgment during the coming weeks.

With a commander in place, Grant now articulated a strategy. Decrying the previous policy of "moving right and left so as to keep between the enemy and our capital," Grant sought instead to adopt an aggressive posture in the Valley. He told first Hunter and then Sheridan to put themselves "south of the enemy and follow him to the death." Lincoln pronounced this view of affairs "exactly right" but advised Grant that such a plan "will neither be done nor attempted unless you watch over it every day and hour and force it." Of course Sheridan, not Grant, would bear this burden. In addition to demolishing Early's army, Grant charged Sheridan with eliminating the Shenandoah Valley as a Confederate military resource. "It is not desirable that the buildings be destroyed," Grant advised. But the residents of the Valley should learn the smell of burning crops and the sight of empty pastures and paddocks so that Virginia's breadbasket could no longer support grayclad soldiers on either side of the Blue Ridge.

Once Sheridan had dispensed with armed opposition and laid waste to the Valley's agriculture, his final task, as explained by Grant, would be to capture the rail lines leading east from Charlottesville and Lynchburg toward Richmond. Once this was accomplished, Robert E. Lee's supply routes would confront near-fatal constriction and Sheridan could approach the Confederate capital from the west to complete the virtual entrapment of the Army of Northern Virginia.

Sheridan thus inherited a tall assignment in a geographic region where Union success of any variety had been rare. He also learned at an early date of another important strategic consideration when he met with Secretary Stanton on his way north. The secretary impressed upon him the dire political repercussions of a defeat near the capital—the administration faced a doubtful election in the fall, and it could not afford another protracted incursion across the Potomac. So, while Grant told Sheridan to win, Stanton warned Sheridan not to lose.

"Little Phil" arrived at Monocacy Junction near Frederick on August 6. Grant met him at the depot, handed him the instructions originally drafted for Hunter, and admonished the young Buckeye to receive direction from "no live man" but Grant himself. The army had pressed forward to Halltown, near Harpers Ferry, under Grant's orders. Sheridan caught up with it there on August 7, the same day the Middle Military Division officially commenced its existence.

Sheridan usually elicited vivid, if not flattering, physical descriptions from first-time viewers. "I sized him up as small of stature and weighing about 135 pounds," wrote a newspaper correspondent, exaggerating the general's weight by ten percent. "His head was abnormally large with projecting bumps which from a phrenologist's view denoted combativeness. His body and arms were long while his pedals were disproportionately short, 'duck legs' in fact. His eyes were black and penetrating. . . . Hard service in the field, and the absence of the razor gave him the appearance of a man 45 years of age." The president shared this impression. Sheridan, thought Lincoln, was "a brown, chunky little chap, not enough neck to hang him, and such long arms that if his ankles itch he can scratch them without stooping."

This peculiar-looking man came to the Valley with experience as a staff officer, colonel of cavalry, and division commander in the West. His reputation soared in the spring of 1864 when, at the head of Meade's cavalry, he conducted a number of large-scale mounted operations that resulted, among lesser accomplishments, in the death of "Jeb" Stuart. The Valley assignment would be, however, his first test as the leader of any army.

That army, consisting of three corps of infantry and one of cavalry, would be known, albeit unofficially until the fall, as the Army of the Shenandoah. Its best troops belonged to the Sixth Corps, dispatched from the Army of the Potomac in July to help rescue Washington from Early's menace. The corps included three divisions and was led by Major General Horatio Gouverneur Wright. Wright's men had campaigned strenuously since the spring and appeared "badly demoralized" to some observers. Wright, though competent, had rarely distinguished himself in combat.

The Eighth Corps, previously known as the Army of West Virginia, hailed almost entirely from the Mountain State or Ohio. A New England officer described these Westerners as "in a fagged-out . . . condition, ragged, famished, discouraged, sulky, and half of them in ambulances. They have been marched to tatters . . . besides being overwhelmed and beaten." Ohioan George Crook, a friend of Sheridan's since their days together at West Point, led the two-division corps. An observer considered Crook "homely in aspect" and possessed of a long nose "somewhat of a Jewish character." Known for his keen vision that earned him the nickname "Gray Eagle," Crook exercised solid, dispassionate military judgment that led one of his officers generously to characterize him as the brains of Sheridan's army.

Sheridan's third infantry corps landed in Virginia by way of Louisiana and the Red River Campaign. The Nineteenth Corps, thirty-five regiments divided between two divisions, originally steered for Petersburg from the Gulf, but the crisis in the Valley prompted Grant to divert them northward. These troops enjoyed steady leadership at the corps level under Brigadier General William H. Emory, whose sandy-colored hair earned him the sobriquet "Old Brick Top." No one could

Major General Horatio Gouverneur Wright

mistake the Nineteenth Corps for a crack outfit, but at least it did not share the legacy of defeat in the East that burdened its comrades.

The army's mounted arm provided Sheridan his staunchest component. No other field force during the Civil War enjoyed a higher ratio of cavalry to infantry and artillery. Twenty-nine regiments in three divisions rode with Sheridan under the overall command of Brigadier General Alfred Thomas Archimedes Torbert. The Delaware native had brought his own and, at Sheridan's request, Brigadier General James H. Wilson's divisions from the Army of the Potomac. Torbert also inherited Crook's cavalry under Major General William Woods Averell, and although Averell ranked Torbert, Sheridan selected his former subordinate for corps command. Torbert presented a less-than-inspiring appearance. Short, bowlegged, and narrow-eyed, one witness thought the general projected "a manner suggestive of a lack of manly vigor." Skilled subordinates like Brigadier General Wesley Merritt, at the head of Torbert's old division, and Brigadier General George Armstrong Custer, a brigade commander, largely compensated for their superior's shortcomings.

Twelve batteries of artillery distributed among the infantry corps completed the army's composition. Estimates of Federal strength at the outset of the campaign vary widely. Sheridan reported twenty-six thousand in his memoirs, but that figure now seems low. Absent one division of the Nineteenth Corps that had not yet arrived, the Army of the Shenandoah counted roughly forty thousand men of all arms on August 7. This was by far the largest Union force ever assembled in the Shenandoah Valley. More importantly, it outnumbered Early's veterans nearly three to one. General Grant had pledged to Sheridan that he would "leave you, as far as possible, to act on your own judgment, and not embarrass you with orders and instructions." Grant would keep his promise, and the impending campaign would belong wholly to Little Phil and his officers and men.

Grant's instructions of August 5 directing the army to concentrate in the vicinity of Harpers Ferry forced Early to withdraw his scattered troops from north of the Potomac. During the next six weeks, Sheridan and Early would conduct a "mimic war" of marching, maneuvering, and skirmishing that resulted in little more than widespread public criticism of the Federal commander. Sheridan established his headquarters at the old paymaster's residence for the Harpers Ferry Armory

Sheridan and His Cavalry Commanders (from left: Brigadier General Wesley Merritt, Brigadier General David McMurtrie Gregg, Sheridan, Brigadier General Henry Eugene Davies, Brigadier General James Harrison Wilson, Brigadier General Alfred Thomas Archimedes Torbert)

and prepared his men for an advance. After receiving a comprehensive lesson on the geography of the Valley from Lieutenant John R. Meigs of his staff, Sheridan set his army in motion on August 10.

The Federals marched toward Berryville, a village south of Halltown and east of Winchester. By so doing, they blocked

Snicker's and Ashby's gaps, two possible avenues for Confederate reinforcements, while compelling Early to fall back up the Valley from Bunker Hill. "Old Jube" continued his southward retreat to Fisher's Hill with Sheridan on his heels along the Valley Pike. On August 12 the Federals halted four miles north of Fisher's Hill behind Cedar Creek. In three days of maneuvering, the Yankees had driven Early completely out of the lower Valley. Sheridan, however, had outdistanced both his supplies and expected reinforcements, a predicament amplified on August 13 by Colonel John S. Mosby's ambush of a wagon train near Berryville in the Union rear. Moreover, Sheridan received word from Grant on August 14 that Lee had diverted "two divisions of infantry . . . some cavalry and twenty pieces of artillery" for service in the Valley. Grant enjoined Sheridan to "be cautious and act now on the defensive" until movements at Petersburg forced Lee to recall these units.

Sheridan quickly recognized the perils of remaining at Cedar Creek and opted to return to Halltown, the only position in the Valley where his left and rear would not be threatened by an attack through passes in the Blue Ridge. The withdrawal began after dark on the fifteenth and continued for a week until the army reoccupied its old trenches on August 22. En route the Federals escaped a possible trap at Front Royal, where Major General Joseph B. Kershaw's Confederate infantry and Major General Fitzhugh Lee's cavalry suddenly appeared. The Unionists then united with Brigadier General Cuvier Grover's division of the Nineteenth Corps and Wilson's cavalry near Winchester. Merritt's troopers also found the opportunity to destroy significant quantities of ripening crops during the retreat, thus addressing one of Grant's campaign objectives. "My retrograde move . . . to Halltown caused considerable alarm in the north," remembered Sheridan, "and loud calls were made for my removal, but I felt confident that my course would be . . . justified . . . being fully convinced that the best course was to bide my time, and wait till I could get the enemy into a position from which he could not escape."

There is no reason at the distance of a century and a quarter to quarrel with Sheridan's thinking. Supplies were short, support far distant, and a powerful enemy column menaced the Federal rear. Grant ordered his subordinate to act defensively, and the Halltown line indisputably offered the best location for such a posture. Sheridan told Halleck that he "thought it best to be prudent," and as Wesley Merritt pointed out, it is ironic that the circumspect Ohioan would gain a reputation for recklessness. Early confidently followed the Federals north, and by returning to the lower Valley offered Sheridan his best chance to sever the Confederate supply line and thrash the Army of the Valley. During the next week, Sheridan wrestled with numerous reports of Confederate reinforcements and attempted to sift fact from rumor. In the process, he missed an opportunity to assail Kershaw's isolated division at Charles Town while Early led the rest of his army up the Potomac.

The troops, blissfully unaware of the larger strategic picture, jokingly called themselves "Harper's Weekly," in reference to their return to the Ferry. The retreat, however, had not punctured their inflating morale. "Sheridan's army is in splendid condition, well in hand and manifesting the greatest anxiety for a fight," reported Colonel Norton P. Chipman of the War Department. "There is a feeling of entire confidence in their leader, and regiments talk about being able to whip brigades." Such testimony barely two weeks after Sheridan's arrival bespeaks a remarkable transformation among men so recently thought to be dispirited.

Sheridan's active reconnaissance convinced him in late August that indeed only one Confederate infantry division had joined Early. Consequently, the Federals advanced on August 28 and within a week assumed a new position between Berryville and Summit Point. Early countered with a shift to Winchester, and for a fortnight the armies distantly glowered at one another across Opequon Creek.

Grant and Sheridan communicated frequently during these two weeks. The latter explained that he had learned of Early's intention to return Kershaw's division to Petersburg and would wait until that moment to resume the offensive. "I would not have you make an attack with the advantage against you, but would prefer just the course you seem to be pursuing," replied Grant. Early confined his activities to dismantling the B&O Railroad and, despite the protests of company officials, Sheridan refused to risk his army to prevent such limited enemy success. He sought not merely to react to Early's initiatives, but to eliminate his opponent's army. Mindful, however, of Stanton's injunctions against hazarding a disaster on election eve, he would not go forward until relative troop strengths justified the attempt.

Although this period of the campaign produced nothing of strategic importance, Sheridan continued to impress his officers and men. "I like Sheridan immensely," averred Colonel Charles Russell Lowell of the cavalry. "Whether he succeeds or fails, he is the first General I have seen who puts as much heart and time and thought into his work as if he were doing it for his own exclusive profit." Tactically, the Union cavalry maintained control of the ground in front of the infantry line and kept close watch on Early's whereabouts. "The careful restless handling of those horsemen by our General whose skill we are now beginning to appreciate, has never been surpassed," enthused a New Englander.

Two other contemporary opinions of Sheridan's performance deserve consultation. Jubal Early drew precisely the wrong impression of his adversary in mid-September: "The events of the last month had satisfied me that the commander opposed to me was without enterprise, and possessed an excessive caution which amounted to timidity," he later wrote. Events would soon underscore Old Jube's miscalculation.

Grant's assessment is more difficult to decipher. Although never demanding that Sheridan abandon the defensive, Grant gave indications of a wish that his lieutenant would strike a blow. "What we want is prompt and active movements after the enemy," he reminded Sheridan. On September 15, the general-in-chief left City Point for the Valley, where he would meet with Sheridan and propose a way to end the impasse. While Grant journeyed north, Sheridan obtained the key to his campaign. Using a slave courier to communicate with a loyal townswoman, Sheridan discovered that Kershaw's division had departed Winchester. So when Grant arrived in Charles Town on the sixteenth with a plan of battle tucked in his pocket, Sheridan made it instantly clear that he required no external prodding to spring into action. "I saw there were but two words of instruction necessary," remembered Grant. "Go in!"

The scheme Grant approved called for a strong Federal force to slice south of Winchester to Newtown and cut Early off from a retreat up the Valley. This proposal conformed with Grant's general preference articulated in August. On September 18, however, Averell informed Sheridan that Early had marched half his infantry toward Martinsburg, leaving merely two divisions near Winchester. Presented with an opportunity to overwhelm a divided enemy, Sheridan formulated a new plan that called for a double envelopment designed to eliminate six isolated brigades under Major General Stephen Dodson Ramseur and Brigadier General Gabriel C. Wharton. While the Sixth and Nineteenth corps pounded the Confederate front, Averell and Merritt would sweep in from the north as Crook blocked the Valley Pike to the south. With a numerical superiority of more than three to one, Sheridan envisioned a battle of annihilation.

The Battle of the Opequon, or Third Winchester, turned out to be something less than decisive, although the outcome clearly favored the Union. Sloppy planning by Sheridan, disappointing performances by some of his subordinates, and tenacious fighting by desperate Confederates robbed a solid conception of total success.

Sheridan predicated his strategy on the need to strike Ramseur and Wharton before Major Generals John B. Gordon and Robert E. Rodes could reappear on the scene with their divisions. Ramseur's position lay at the western end of a long, narrow defile called the Berryville Canyon. The Union commander unwisely ordered both Wright and Emory to traverse the canyon on a single road, ignoring alternative routes and assuring a time-consuming approach to the Confederate position. Wright exacerbated the problem by disobeying Sheridan's explicit order to park all Sixth Corps regimental wagons at Summit Point. General Emory, therefore, encountered a massive traffic jam at the mouth of the canyon created by Wright's vehicles.

The Federal army required the entire morning to reach a position from which to launch its attack, and by then Early had reconcentrated his scattered divisions. The Union cavalry on Sheridan's right, although unencumbered by clogged roads or significant Rebel opposition, likewise made slow progress. Near midday, Sheridan at last deployed two divisions of the Sixth Corps on his left and the Nineteenth Corps on his right. Brigadier General David A. Russell's division of Wright's command remained in reserve. Sheridan ordered Wright to advance using the Berryville Pike as his axis of approach. Unfortunately, the road quickly bent south from its east-west alignment, and a large gap opened between the right of the Sixth Corps following the road and the Nineteenth Corps farther north. Rodes's division plunged into this breach and wreaked havoc among the blue brigades before Russell's division ended the crisis with a perfectly executed counterattack that Wright called "the turning point in the conflict." The division commander himself fell dead from a shell fragment that passed through his heart, depriving Sheridan of one of his bravest soldiers.

The only uncommitted troops now on the field belonged to Crook. Sheridan squandered his reserves, however, by leaving them far to the rear without orders and totally out of position to influence the fighting. Eventually, the Westerners did move up on the army's right in support of Emory's weary men. Colonel Isaac H. Duval's division crossed Red Bud Run and mounted an effective flank attack that marked the beginning of the end for Early at Winchester. After the war, Sheridan claimed credit for this maneuver, but Crook steadfastly maintained that "the idea of turning the enemy's flank never occurred to him, but I took the responsibility on my own shoulders."

Brigadier General Emory Upton, Russell's successor and himself severely wounded, built upon Crook's momentum. He continued to press the beleaguered Confederates, at times leading his division from a stretcher. Sheridan recognized that the time had come for a last grand effort. Union cavalry pressured Early's left, north of Winchester, and by dint of personal exertion

Battle of Third Winchester or Opequon—Federal Assault on the Morning of September 19, 1864

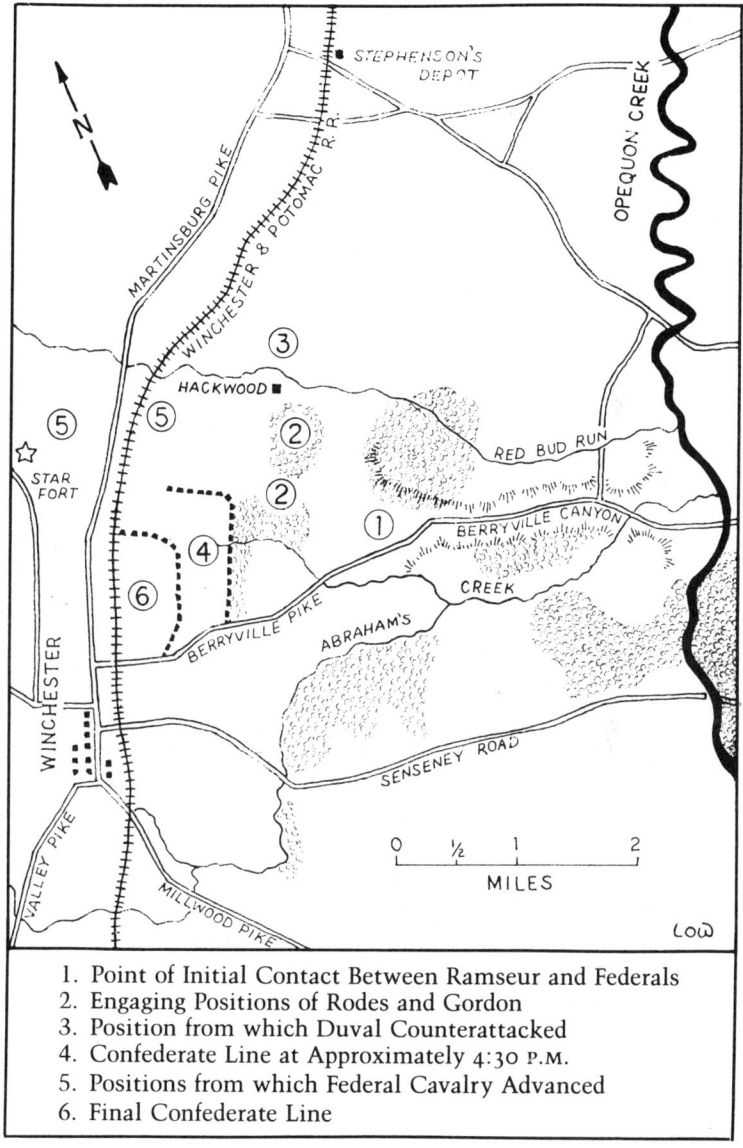

1. Point of Initial Contact Between Ramseur and Federals
2. Engaging Positions of Rodes and Gordon
3. Position from which Duval Counterattacked
4. Confederate Line at Approximately 4:30 P.M.
5. Positions from which Federal Cavalry Advanced
6. Final Confederate Line

Battle of Third Winchester or the Opequon, September 19, 1864 the army commander marshalled his sweat-soaked infantry to the east. "Riding at a terrible speed along the whole of our extended skirmish line, wheeling out from the storm of bullets . . . and pausing as he passed between the brigades to exclaim with eloquent profanity, 'Crook and Averell are on their left and rear—we've got 'em bagged by ———,' " Sheridan orchestrated the final attack. Another awestruck observer remembered that "Little Phil was no tongue-tied angel when the spirit of battle was on him. Stupidity, cowardice, incompetence, and panic would enrage him to such a pitch that strange, novel picturesque oaths, made upon the spot, would burst from him spontaneously."

The simultaneous assaults proved too much for the exhausted Confederates, who streamed up the Valley and into the gathering darkness. Wilson's cavalry abetted their escape by failing to test the thin resistance in their front, southeast of Winchester. Had they pushed forward, it is likely that the Federal troopers would have caught Early's fleeing troops above town.

The Battle of the Opequon resulted, nonetheless, in important accomplishments for the Union cause. In addition to routing the Confederate army, the victory restored the lower Valley to Federal control and permanently relieved Maryland, Pennsylvania, and Washington from the threat of invasion. The B&O Railroad and the Chesapeake and Ohio Canal also reopened, to the satisfaction of Yankee businessmen. Most importantly, Northern morale soared dramatically after the battle. The *New York Tribune* exclaimed: "Hurrah for Phil Sheridan! And for his gallant army! We remember no victory in this War which has more suddenly awakened the sympathies of the North; nor one which has been welcomed with more enthusiastic delight." Grant viewed the battle as "the most effective campaign argument made in the canvass."

The victory also proved to be a personal triumph for Sheridan. He received promotion to brigadier general in the regular army and permanent command of the Middle Military Division. Perhaps more critically for the future, his troops had learned to adore him. "Since the time of McClellan," testified a

Vermonter, "it had been a point of pride with the Brigade not to cheer its officers; but [after Winchester] tumultuous hurrahs came unbidden from the bottom of every heart and conventional restraint was forgotten." Sheridan's personal courage, ability to respond to fluid battlefield conditions, and skillful use of combined cavalry and infantry contributed to the successful outcome. So too did Jubal Early, who foolishly placed his outnumbered army in a position to be destroyed. The engagement clearly validated Sheridan's insistence upon waiting to strike a diminished enemy, both for what was and what might have been achieved at Winchester. Had it not been for the faulty preparation by the Union commander and indifferent or incompetent execution by several of his lieutenants, the Battle of the Opequon might have ended the Valley campaign.

Sheridan began his pursuit of the beaten Confederates at 5:00 A.M. on September 20. By day's end, the army had covered twenty southbound miles to Strasburg. The Federals discovered Early dug in behind Tumbling Run along the range of ridges running parallel to the Valley Pike known collectively as Fisher's Hill. This position "seemed to us soldiers perfectly impregnable," remembered one Yankee, "and we could not see how Sheridan was going to rout him from it."

The general called his corps commanders to a council of war after dark. Everyone agreed that a frontal attack was out of the question. Sheridan then suggested an effort against Early's right. Such a conception defied logic because the Confederates held this portion of their line—anchored on Massanutten Mountain and the North Fork of the Shenandoah River—in great strength. Wisely, no one endorsed Sheridan's idea. Crook then proposed a turning movement to the west, around Early's left. Wright and Emory rejected this plan as well, but Sheridan liked it. He liked it so much, in fact, that after the war he claimed credit for devising it. "It was fully understood by every one at Corps Headquarters . . . that Crook had suggested this movement," stated Eighth Corps chief of artillery Captain Henry A. Du Pont. Just as with Winchester, Sheridan's postwar quest for glory manufactured an acrimonious controversy where none had existed on the battlefield.

Brigadier General George Crook

The final element of Union strategy at Fisher's Hill involved the cavalry. Sheridan detached Merritt's division to join Wilson's in the Page (or Luray) Valley, east of Massanutten, to push south and then west through New Market Gap. Although Merritt perceived his mission as a turning movement, Sheridan viewed it as an attempt to block Early's escape once the blue infantry had driven the Confederates from Fisher's Hill. Once again, Little Phil aimed for the total ruination of his opponent. The cavalry cantered up the Page Valley on September 21 with General Torbert at the head. Wright and Emory demonstrated actively in Early's front while Crook remained concealed from Confederate observation posts on Massanutten. Late in the day, elements of the Sixth Corps seized advantageous ground in front of Fisher's Hill while Crook prepared to move out after sunset.

A biographer of Sheridan calls the Battle of Fisher's Hill "one of the best examples of 'grand tactics' in the history of the war." Crook's march along Little North Mountain caught the enemy completely by surprise on September 22, setting the stage for a devastating attack against the Confederate left. Sheridan skillfully employed the Sixth and Nineteenth corps after Crook piled into Early's overmatched defenders, and the battle degenerated into a rout. "Run boys, run!" screamed the blue commander. "Don't wait to form! Don't let 'em stop! If you can't run, then holler!" Only the dismal performance of the Union cavalry robbed Sheridan of the chance to make Fisher's Hill a decisive victory. Torbert's troopers to the east had encountered two small Southern brigades at Milford on September 21 and then, unknown to Sheridan, timidly retreated down the Valley to Front Royal. "I have been unable to account satisfactorily for Torbert's failure," Sheridan wrote. "Had General Torbert driven [their] cavalry or turned the defile and reached New Market, I have no doubt but that we would have captured the entire rebel army."

Nevertheless, the triumph on September 22, especially when viewed in conjunction with the battle three days before, solidified Sheridan's glowing reputation. Early's losses at the two engagements totaled more than one-third of the entire

Confederate strength. The moral and political fruits harvested
at the Opequon increased after Fisher's Hill. With the exception of Torbert's irresolute behavior, the Federals executed a
tactical masterpiece along Tumbling Run. "Keep on and your
good work will cause the fall of Richmond," Grant encouraged
his young lieutenant. "We all absolutely believed that Sheridan
was invincible," echoed a man in the ranks.

Grover's division of the Nineteenth Corps led the infantry
pursuit on the night of September 22–23. Sheridan drove his
foot soldiers mercilessly. "Neither man-flesh or horseflesh
had any consideration from him when garnering the fruits of
such a victory," wrote a weary New Yorker. Of course cavalry,
not infantry, held the key to catching the Confederates. With
Torbert out of the picture east of Massanutten, Sheridan
looked to Averell's troopers to show the way. Averell, however,
seemed more interested in harvesting the spoils of battle
at Fisher's Hill than capitalizing on Early's discomfiture. He
failed to arrive in Woodstock until midday September 23, more
than eight hours after the infantry reached that village,
whereupon Sheridan furiously ordered him to close with the
Confederates: "I do not advise rashness, but I do desire . . . actual fighting with necessary casualties, before you retire. There
must now be no backing and filling by you."

Despite this positive injunction, Averell failed to press Early's
fleeing fugitives and calmly bivouacked that evening near
Hawkinsburg. Sheridan promptly sacked him. "I thought . . .
that the interest of the service would be subserved by removing one whose growing indifference might render the best laid
plans inoperative," Sheridan later explained. He replaced
Averell with one of his brigade commanders, Colonel William
H. Powell. Historians disagree not only about why Sheridan
fired Averell, but also about the question of whether the dismissal was even warranted. Averell, like Fifth Corps commander Gouverneur K. Warren at Five Forks the following
spring, enraged his emotional general by flunking at a critical
moment. Moreover, both officers set the stage for their remov-
als with contentious attitudes and checkered battle records.
On September 23, Sheridan needed an outlet for frustrations

Brigadier General William Woods Averell

caused as much by Torbert as by Averell. Unlike his fellow cavalry chieftains, Averell shared scant legacy with Little Phil or the Army of the Potomac and thus found himself on his way to Wheeling and out of the war.

Meanwhile, the resilient Army of the Valley quickly recovered its organization and took refuge at the western foot of the Blue Ridge. Sheridan followed as far as Mount Crawford and Harrisonburg, where he spent the next two weeks destroying or removing supplies in the upper Valley. On September 30, Grant transferred James H. Wilson to take charge of Sherman's cavalry in Georgia. Sheridan's selection of Custer as Wilson's replacement strengthened his mounted arm more significantly than had his exile of Averell. "While Wilson had command of the 3d Division . . . scarcely a member of it would acknowledge his connection with it, but now it was very different," stated an Ohio trooper. "Every member felt proud to be known as one of Custer's division."

"The question that now presented itself," wrote Sheridan in his memoirs, "was whether or not I should follow the enemy to Brown's gap, where he still held fast, drive him out and advance on Charlottesville and Gordonsville." Thus far in the campaign, Sheridan had partially achieved two of Grant's three original objectives. He had badly damaged Early's army at Winchester and Fisher's Hill, and made some progress in ravishing the Valley. Wrecking the Virginia Central Railroad east of the Blue Ridge would score a military hat trick that, together with Sherman's capture of Atlanta, might bring the end of the war into view. The administration and Northern public opinion echoed the lieutenant general's desire for Sheridan to cross the mountains and move east toward Richmond, but Sheridan declined to do so. He harbored concerns for supplying his army on the march across the Blue Ridge, protecting a new supply line east of the mountains along the Orange & Alexandria Railroad, and ensuring the security of the lower Valley. Moreover, Early might receive reinforcements from Richmond, argued the Union commander, and overwhelm the diminished Federal force working its way east from Gordonsville. Better, thought Sheridan, to complete the ruination of the Valley, retain a small contingent near the Potomac, and return the bulk of his troops to Grant at Petersburg.

Sheridan displayed remarkable unselfishness in this analysis. Rarely do successful army commanders, especially ambitious ones, champion the dissolution of their own implements of glory. The fact remains, however, that Sheridan erred in his thinking. Confederate guerrilla operations did pose a real threat to any extended Union supply line, but he possessed the firepower to cope with Southern partisans. Grant conducted offensive operations at Petersburg that promised to prevent Lee from detaching more troops to Early, and Sheridan certainly could have found the means to feed his men as they traversed the mountains.

Writers later speculated that had Sheridan followed Grant's wishes the war would have ended in the fall. This conclusion may be optimistic, but James H. Wilson's belief that Sheridan "might have continued the pursuit till he had driven Early back on Lee" seems irrefutable. Grant, however, bears partial responsibility for this missed opportunity. Instead of insisting upon the execution of his solid strategic thinking, the general-in-chief cancelled orders to repair the Orange & Alexandria Railroad on October 2 and endorsed Sheridan's overly conservative recommendations. Sheridan received Grant's approval on October 5, and the next morning commenced his withdrawal down the Valley. "I noted in the general's staff little of that lightheartedness usual among officers in lax moments on returning from a successful campaign," observed a journalist. "I could well fancy how distasteful to their military pride must have been the surrender of the territory conquered after such mature preparations . . . hard fighting, and heavy loss of life."

Sheridan, however, intended to leave the Valley as thoroughly conquered as if his army had remained in occupation. Between October 6 and 8 the Federals systematically burned barns, mills, and crops, inflicting more than twenty million dollars in damage. According to one Ohio trooper, "the burning details were scattered for miles on either flank, [and] as we came to the top [of] each gentle swell . . . [and] look[ed] around, it was no uncommon sight to see at least fifty barns on fire. . . . A heavy cloud of smoke hung over the whole valley like a pall." Some of the Northerners found their incendiary work distasteful and perhaps counterproductive. "If ever troops

found an incentive to strike vigorous blows for their 'homes
and firesides' it was those who fought [our] destructions,"
thought a Pennsylvanian. Sheridan placed a different, more
modern twist on the operation: "I am sure there is more mercy
in destroying supplies than in killing their young men, which a
continuance of the war would entail. If I had a barnful of
wheat and a son, I would much sooner lose the barn and
wheat. . . . The question was, must we destroy their supplies or
kill their young men? We chose the former."

"The Burning" exceeded every such undertaking of the Civil
War save Sherman's "March to the Sea." There can be no
doubt that the devastation contributed to Confederate deser-
tion by prompting sons of Valley families to return home to
help their kin survive the winter. There is, however, persua-
sive evidence that much of the Valley escaped the flames.
Sheridan's arsonists did their worst on farms adjacent to the
Valley Pike, while the property of citizens lying off the beaten
path remained largely unscathed. As a philosophical country-
man in Woodstock told the Yankees: "You folks don't work the
thing right . . . there are hundreds of folks living over in the
bottoms, that you never see . . . where there are hundreds of
acres of splendid corn untouched, while we that live on the
pike are literally stripped of everything."

In addition to this lack of thoroughness, Sheridan's destruc-
tive withdrawal down the Valley met with interference from
Confederate cavalry. Major General Thomas L. Rosser, possessed of an undersized brigade and an oversized reputation as
the "Savior of the Valley," orchestrated the harassment. On the
evening of October 8, an exasperated Sheridan ordered Torbert
to "start out at daylight and whip the rebel cavalry or get
whipped." He called for a total commitment of Custer's and
Merritt's divisions and, mindful of Torbert's failure in the Page
Valley, told his cavalry chief that he would personally observe
the action from nearby Round Hill.

A Confederate referred to the ensuing Battle of Tom's Brook
as the "greatest disaster that ever befell our cavalry." The
gray horsemen managed to hold their ground for three hours
before superior numbers and bold tactics sent Rosser and

Federal Cavalry laying Waste to the Lower Valley, October 1864

Major General Lunsford L. Lomax tearing twenty-six miles up the Valley in retreat. The Confederates left eleven guns on the field, making thirty-two pieces of artillery lost since September 19. Union casualties numbered fewer than sixty. The greatest benefit of the victory on October 9 was its negative impact on Confederate cavalry morale. The Southern troopers' reluctance to confront their Yankee counterparts again would manifest itself ten days later at Cedar Creek.

The Battle of Tom's Brook convinced Sheridan that the war in the Valley had ended. "I believe that a rebel advance down this Valley will not take place," he wired Grant on October 11. Little Phil halted Crook and Emory in their familiar positions north of Cedar Creek, but directed Wright to continue toward Front Royal and Ashby's Gap on the first leg of a return trip to Petersburg. He also ordered Powell's cavalry to execute a raid against the railroads at Gordonsville and Charlottesville. The raid, an obvious sop to Grant, came to nothing; Powell had failed utterly in his mission by October 14. Sheridan recalled the unsuccessful troopers, who in reality enjoyed little chance to reach Gordonsville in such limited strength. Wright then resumed his eastward trek, temporarily suspended by Sheridan in deference to a communiqué of caution from Grant.

Sheridan now operated under a serious misapprehension. Completely losing track of his opponent, he believed that Early's main army rested somewhere between Brown's Gap and Waynesboro, more than sixty miles south of Cedar Creek. Only a series of fortuitous events saved the Federals from a calamity worse than the one that would befall them on October 19.

The first lucky episode originated in Washington. Grant sent an order to Sheridan, through Halleck, on October 11, requesting that he threaten Gordonsville and Charlottesville with a raid. Sheridan, as we know, had anticipated such a request and already dispatched Powell to do Grant's bidding. Halleck, however, twisted Grant's order to fit his own strategic preference. "General Grant wishes a position taken far enough south to serve as a base for future operations upon Gordonsville and Charlottesville," Halleck informed Sheridan on October 12.

"It must be strongly fortified and provisioned. Some point in the vicinity of Manassas Gap would seem best suited for all purposes."

These were Halleck's words, not Grant's. They had the salutary effect, however, of prompting Sheridan to halt the Alexandria-bound Sixth Corps. If Grant wanted to establish a fortified base at Manassas Gap, the Valley commander would not do so without Wright's veterans. Thus, by attempting to manipulate affairs to his own strategic liking, Halleck unwittingly retained the Sixth Corps within marching distance of Cedar Creek.

Jubal Early abetted this situation by conducting an ill-advised reconnaissance-in-force. The Confederates, of course, were not in the upper Valley as Sheridan presumed, but had marched down the Pike to within a few miles of the unsuspecting Yankees. On October 13, Old Jube probed the Federal position on Abram Stickley's farm and engaged Colonel Joseph Thoburn's division of the Eighth Corps with some tactical advantage. The combat, however, alerted Sheridan to Early's presence, and the Union commander ordered Wright to rejoin the army. The Sixth Corps filed into camp at noon the following day.

Now that Halleck and Early had unconsciously conspired to reunite the army's infantry, Edwin Stanton succeeded in depriving it of its leader. On October 13 the secretary of war requested a meeting with Sheridan to resolve the vexing disagreements regarding the fate of the Valley army. "It was my intention to attack the enemy as soon as the Sixth Corps reached me," Sheridan later revealed, but Early's withdrawal to Fisher's Hill persuaded him that the Confederates posed no immediate threat. Little Phil simply could not believe that after the thrashings he administered to Early at Winchester, Fisher's Hill, and Tom's Brook his opponent would dare to attack his concentrated army. Therefore, Sheridan accepted Stanton's invitation to confer in Washington.

He departed for the capital on the evening of October 15, leaving Wright in temporary command with explicit instructions for vigilance. Merritt's cavalry division escorted Sheridan to Front Royal with orders to accompany Powell's troopers from there on another, stronger raid against the railroads. Early's next miscalculation, however, revoked these plans. The Confederate commander hoped to intimidate the Federals at Cedar Creek by signaling a bogus message announcing the imminent approach of James Longstreet's entire corps. The Federals intercepted the transmission, as Early knew they would, and on the sixteenth Wright relayed its contents to Sheridan, who correctly identified the ploy, but as a precaution cancelled the mounted raid. He returned his cavalry to Cedar Creek and admonished Wright to "make your position strong."

Sheridan arrived in Washington on the seventeenth, and within four hours convinced the secretary of war that most of the Army of the Shenandoah should be forwarded to Grant in Southside Virginia. Accompanied by two out-of-shape engineer officers charged with erecting a defensive line in the lower Valley, Sheridan quickly boarded a special train for Martinsburg, whence he would ride south to rejoin his men.

Despite Sheridan's warnings, Wright had not crafted a formidable position behind Cedar Creek. In fairness to the acting commander, the terrain offered poor prospects for defense. Abrupt hills and valleys tended to segregate units beyond immediate mutual support, while concealed approaches from Fisher's Hill made it difficult to advance pickets sufficiently without risking their capture. Moreover, neither the creek nor the North Fork of the Shenandoah River presented an insurmountable obstacle to enemy passage. Union Brigadier General Lewis A. Grant characterized the army's posture as "almost defenseless," and he was right. Sheridan had not chosen the Cedar Creek line with a view toward serious resistance, believing Early to be incapable of significant aggression. Wright did little to mitigate this potentially disastrous situation.

The Eighth Corps occupied the army's left with Thoburn's division on an isolated knoll near the confluence of the creek and river. Emory's men built trenches upstream on the creek overlooking the Valley Pike, while the Sixth Corps encamped on the Union right. Custer and Merritt patrolled west of the Sixth Corps on the ground most likely to attract Confederate

Brigadier General William Hemsley Emory

attention. Wright erred by virtually ignoring Sheridan's orders to "close in Colonel Powell [from Front Royal] . . . look well to your ground, and be well prepared." The acting commander shifted only one of Powell's three brigades upstream on the

river to make a tenuous connection with Crook's left. This
oversight helped Early succeed on October 19.

Reconnaissance on the eighteenth reinforced Wright's false
sense of security. Neither Torbert nor Colonel Thomas A.
Harris, a brigade commander in Thoburn's division, sighted
the Confederates all day. Harris claimed to have explored as far
as the enemy's old camps at Fisher's Hill, which, obviously, he
had not done. To his credit, Wright did notice suspicious civilians observing the Union lines from Hupp's Hill, south of
Cedar Creek. He prudently ordered the Nineteenth Corps to go
out early the next day to verify the absence of Confederates,
instructions the Federals never had a chance to obey.

The Battle of Cedar Creek, considered by some historians as
"second only to Gettysburg as the most glamorous Union victory of the Civil War," derives its notoriety from the remarkable turnaround that marked its course. The engagement,
pitting some thirty-one thousand Federals against half as
many Confederates, may be divided conveniently into three
distinct phases. From first light to mid-morning, Early's army
drove each Union infantry corps, one after the other, from its
chosen position. Between 10:00 A.M. and 4:00 P.M., a period
of maneuvering and relative quiet pervaded the field. The
final phase, beginning late in the afternoon, consisted of a po-
tent Union counterattack resulting in the total rout of the
Southern army.

The Confederates owed their morning success to a daring
nocturnal march around the Federal left and a surprise assault
at daybreak. The role that Union generalship played in this
achievement has generated considerable controversy. It ap-
pears, however, that a combination of several factors led to the
Federal debacle. Horatio Wright cannot escape primary blame
for the fate of his army on the morning of October 19. He man-
ifestly apprehended no danger to his left flank and said as
much to Sheridan in a message delivered three days earlier: "I
shall hold on here until the enemy's movements are developed
and shall only fear an attack on my right, which I shall make
every preparation for guarding against and resisting." Sheridan
responded with his order to bring Powell up from Front Royal.

Crook, whose westerners would be victimized first by Early's unwelcome reveille, testified that he warned Wright of the inadequate picket line on his front and that the general promised to rectify the weakness. Wright retained Merritt and Custer more than five miles from the river, however, and kept most of Powell's troopers far to the north. In these actions, Wright merely reflected the nearly universal opinion entertained in the Federal camps that Early would not risk an offensive. Neither the absent Sheridan nor "Gray Eagle" Crook foresaw the Confederates' eventual contrivance; their warnings to look out for the left stemmed more from caution than from prescience.

What pickets Crook did post lay too close to the main line, and the picket reserves dozed contentedly as Early's bombshell exploded. The inherently weak positions occupied by the divisions of Thoburn and Brigadier General Rutherford B. Hayes, together with a dense morning fog, guaranteed that once the unsuspecting Yankees felt the impact of Early's coordinated blows they would have little chance for quick recovery. "Probably no troops in the world," concluded a judicious observer, "would have done any better, situated as they were."

In contrast to their culpability for the initial catastrophe at Cedar Creek, Wright and his lieutenants performed as well as could be expected during the balance of the battle's first stage. General Emory turned out his men under arms before dawn, and, although compelled to abandon their untenable entrenchments, the Nineteenth Corps fought bravely. Emory lost two horses killed beneath him in fifteen minutes. The Sixth Corps battled gamely from high ground northwest of Meadow Brook on the army's right, acting corps commander Brigadier General James B. Ricketts falling wounded. Brigadier General George W. Getty's division then stood firm at the Middletown Cemetery and repulsed several desperate attacks before withdrawing to establish a new line.

General Wright, bleeding from a wound to the chin, energetically directed affairs and salvaged some degree of order from the chaos. More importantly, he instructed most of the cavalry to gallop to the army's left and draw a defensive front east of

the Valley Pike below Middletown. This prudent measure ensured that the most vulnerable Federal flank would be protected and the Northern line of retreat secured.

Suspension of the Confederate attacks coincided closely
with the arrival of Phil Sheridan. Although the general's cele-
brated ride from Winchester belongs as much to American my-
thology as it does to history, the Union commander, in fact,
covered about twelve miles in something less than two hours.
No question exists regarding his valiant effort to rally dispirited fugitives en route, save the language he used to achieve
the metamorphosis: "Boys, turn back; face the other way,"
Sheridan pleaded, according to one sanitized version. Army
surgeon C. H. Parry remembered more vivid rhetoric: "God
damn you, don't cheer me! If you love your country, come up
to the front! God damn you, don't cheer me! There's a lot of
fight in you men yet! Come up, God damn you!"

Sheridan's arrival on the field, heralded by a swelling chorus
of cheers resonating up the Pike, transformed the Northern
army as if by chemical reaction. "Sheridan possessed in a degree unequalled the power of raising in the hearts of his soldiers the sort of enthusiasm that . . . causes men to attempt
impossibilities, and to disregard and overcome obstacles,"
wrote the historian of the Nineteenth Corps. "The men sprang
to their feet and cheered as only men under such circumstances can," remembered a soldier. "Hope and confidence returned at a bound. . . . Now we all burned to attack the enemy,
to drive him back, to retrieve our honor, and sleep in our old
camps that night."

Sheridan recognized the value of his magnetic personality
and enormous popularity with the troops. Detecting Early's intention to renew his advance about midday, Sheridan, "hat in
hand, passed along the entire length of the [Union] infantry
line." Cavalry officer James H. Kidd recalled that the soldiers
issued "a shout that sent a thrill across the valley." Sheridan's
recipe for redemption included showmanship, bravado, and
conscious, selfless exposure to danger. He deftly employed his
personal prestige as a tactical weapon against the enemy.

Did Little Phil appear in the nick of time to rescue the Army of the Shenandoah from oblivion? No. Wright had the situation under control, and Early already had done his worst. Nevertheless, Sheridan made several decisions that irrefutably improved Federal prospects. He wisely opted to fight along the line Getty had established north of Middletown. Using the remainder of the Sixth Corps and Emory's troops, he prolonged this front to the west, strengthened it with some twenty guns, and ordered the construction of breastworks. Early's feeble attack at 1:00 P.M. encountered this barrier and shrank before it. Sheridan also returned Custer's division to the army's right where it could strike Early's flank.

Then the bullet-headed general turned his thoughts to the offensive. Reports from Powell's division near Front Royal, however, indicated the presence of a heavy infantry force marching toward Winchester. "I could not fully believe that such a movement would be undertaken," Sheridan wrote, but he sensibly restrained his brigades until he could safely discredit Powell's rumors. He instructed Merritt to capture an exposed Confederate battery posted at the edge of Middletown; and after personally interrogating the prisoners, he ascertained that the oft-dreaded spector of Longstreet was a mirage. He then ordered a full-scale counterattack.

Sheridan miscalculated by directing the assault to commence with Getty's division on the left of his line. These intrepid veterans faced the strongest part of Early's position and thus suffered severely until the Federal right pivoted into action. Before long the Federals surged irresistibly forward, emphatically sweeping their opponents from the field. Custer's cavalry played a prominent role in driving the Rebels across Cedar Creek and far to the south, but every Union command—even the unfortunate Eighth Corps—contributed to the resounding victory.

Although fighting and maneuvering would continue in the Shenandoah Valley, Cedar Creek marked the end of purposeful Confederate resistance in this theater. Sheridan's army paid dearly for its achievement. Ten brigade, division, or corps commanders fell killed or wounded on October 19, alongside fifty-seven hundred men of lesser rank. The entire campaign cost the Federals nearly seventeen thousand casualties. But the gains seemed worth the price: four major victories, eight thousand casualties inflicted, the Confederate mounted arm destroyed, fifty-eight pieces of artillery captured, and the Valley in ruins.

On the evening of October 23, Assistant Secretary Dana appeared at Sheridan's headquarters. Perhaps reflecting on his well-founded suggestion to Grant barely three months previously, Lincoln's emissary presented Sheridan with a commission as major general in the United States Army. "Sheridan did not say much in reply to my little speech," remembered Dana. "He seemed more interested in resuming his sleep than exchanging compliments."

Such a reaction typified a general who in 1864 sought no great measure of personal recognition. Kudos approaching deification found him nonetheless. Grant told the secretary of war that "turning what had bid fair to be disaster into glorious victory stamped Sheridan what I have always thought him, one of the ablest of generals." Meade, Sherman, Stanton, and Lincoln all echoed this assessment. With the passage of time, Sheridan began to believe his own press clippings and sought to enhance his exalted reputation. "The adulations heaped on him by a grateful nation for his supposed genius turned his head," wrote a bitter George Crook after the war, "which added to his natural disposition, caused him to bloat his little carcass with debauchery and dissipation."

The evolution of Little Phil's ego aside, what combination of factors led to Union victory west of the Blue Ridge in 1864? Does Sheridan deserve the praise he received in the wake of the campaign? Who else warranted a share of the credit for Early's demise?

Responsibility for Northern success begins with Abraham Lincoln. The president gave Grant his undivided confidence and allowed him a sufficient force to clean out the Shenandoah Valley. The general-in-chief, in turn, trusted Sheridan and did not interfere with his subordinate's prerogatives, even when he preferred a different course of action. The competent soldiers and capable officers of the Army of the Shenandoah also deserve considerable praise. Crook, Wright, Custer, Merritt, Upton, Getty, and others enjoyed distinguished moments on the bloody fields of the Opequon, Fisher's Hill, Tom's Brook, and Cedar Creek.

But this campaign belongs more to Sheridan than to any other Northern figure. No general in those days of personal leadership inspired troops more effectively. Moreover, Sheridan shaped a cohesive army out of three disparate commands. He employed cavalry with infantry more skillfully than anyone had done before him. He never knew a moment's indecision on the battlefield and adjusted instantly to changing tactical conditions. Above all, like another great Valley general, he nourished an indomitable will to win and always looked for a decisive victory.

Sheridan also displayed a level of caution and discretion that garnered mixed results. The victory at Winchester vindicated his oft-criticized patience in August and September, but his refusal to pursue Early across the mountains after Fisher's Hill probably prolonged the siege of Petersburg. The Federal tactical performance left something to be desired on every Valley battlefield, and Sheridan's critics invariably explain each Union conquest in terms of Northern numerical superiority. "It is true that he destroyed Early . . . in 1864," wrote James Longstreet, "but that was no great job. Early had no real military capacity." Longstreet's double entendre aside, many historians argue that Sheridan's preponderance of strength guaranteed his ultimate triumph. Such a thesis ignores the record at Sharpsburg, Chancellorsville, and other engagements where Southern armies fought successfully against odds of more than two to one.

Union ascendancy in the 1864 Valley campaign was not inevitable, but Sheridan's personal leadership and the support of the administration and the general-in-chief made it likely. In turn, results on the battlefield greatly increased morale in

the North and contributed to Lincoln's reelection. As Jeffry
Wert observes in his fine study of this phase of the Civil War,
Sheridan's victory removed the Confederacy's last hope of
breaking "Grant's deathgrip on Petersburg . . . [and] insured
Southern defeat in Virginia."

"The Cause of All My Disasters"
Jubal A. Early and the
Undisciplined Valley Cavalry

ROBERT K. KRICK

Two and one-half millennia before the opening of the Shenandoah Valley campaign of 1864, Assyrian military men achieved temporary superiority over their neighbors when they perfected mounted tactics and inaugurated the cavalry arm. When Philip H. Sheridan's horsemen swarmed over Jubal A. Early's at Winchester and Cedar Creek in the fall of 1864, they were marking the end of a long era of mounted combat. Cavalry reached the apex of its importance and usefulness in American military history during the Civil War. Decades of mounted adventuring remained in the future of the Western plains, but large-scale clashes on horseback faded from the American experience when the Confederacy died.

The importance of cavalry during the Civil War left many Confederate leaders fuming over what they perceived to be the ineptitude of the horsemen available to them. Cavalry baiting became virtually endemic throughout the Southern armed forces. The unchallenged leaders in those verbal assaults were Early and D. H. Hill. It was apparently Hill who coined the satirical jibe that swept the armies: "Who ever saw a dead cavalryman?" Hill unleashed a particularly savage sally when he assumed a new command early in 1863. In a published proclamation, he declared that cavalry pickets "who permit themselves to be surprised deserve to die, and the commanding general will spare no efforts to secure them their deserts." Mounted troops bringing in "sensational reports," Hill blustered, would be "court-martialed for cowardice."

Jubal Early took command of Confederate affairs in Virginia's important granary, the Shenandoah Valley, in the summer

of 1864 under the conviction that the cavalry he inherited in
that district resembled those of D. H. Hill's caricature. The to-
pography of the Valley and the brutal numerical odds that
Early faced during the next several months would focus even
more attention than usual on his cavalry arm. A young Vermont soldier among the invaders of the Valley summarized the
effect of geography on operations there in three droll sentences
addressed to his homefolks: "The Shenandoah Valley is a queer
place, and it will not submit to the ordinary rules of military
tactics. Operations are carried on here that Caesar or Napoleon
never dreamed of. Either army can surround the other, and I
believe they both can do it at the same time." Across and
around that complex terrain Early's army moved 1,670 miles
during four and one-half months and fought seventy-five engagements, according to calculations of the careful staff diarist
Jedediah Hotchkiss.

By any gauge, Early was a curmudgeon. He hesitated not at
all in allotting blame to subordinates at all levels. One of his
young brigadiers boasted in a contemporary letter of an unac-
customed compliment from the army commander, and noted
that it was particularly noteworthy coming from "one of the
most cross grained & faultfinding Gens. in the C.S. Army."
Three days after the largest battle of the campaign, "Old Jube"
ground out a lengthy broadside to his men in scathing indictment of their behavior. "I had hoped to have congratulated
you," he began, "[but instead] I have the mortification of announcing to you, that, by your . . . misconduct, all the benefits
of that victory were lost and a serious disaster incurred." In
what must have been a wretchedly unsuccessful effort to stim-
ulate the troops, Early compared them unfavorably to the
"proudly defiant" men under Robert E. Lee in the Petersburg
trenches. The only hope for the Valley men to "again claim
them as comrades," Early announced, was "to erase from your
escutcheons the blemishes which now obscure them."

On the other hand, Early displayed considerable skill under
dreadful conditions in the 1864 Valley campaign. His loyalty
and devotion to the cause and his eagerness to fulfill Lee's injunctions reveal a man doing his level best with what was at

hand. The "Buttermilk Rangers," as Early called his Valley cavalry—implying a fondness for foraging and domestic scenes far from the cannon's roar—clearly performed at inadequate levels on many occasions. When the general told Lee that the weakness and inefficiency of his cavalry "has been the cause of all my disasters," was he offering a valid judgment? Just how bad was the Valley cavalry in 1864?

A first casual, almost reflexive, impression of cavalry operations might suggest the notion that discipline among Civil War cavalry units was not quite as important as among their counterparts in infantry and artillery service. Cavalry's role customarily involved smaller groups, in widely separated locations, requiring less of the shoulder-to-shoulder training and regimen so necessary to tactical evolutions of the other arms. In fact, of course, precisely that dispersal and lack of large-scale, visually controllable action made discipline absolutely essential to the successful functioning of cavalry. The disciplinary needs of cavalry units were magnified later in the war as cavalrymen more and more often fought dismounted as "Mounted Infantry," an outgrowth of one of the war's evolutionary tactical developments.

The fabulously inefficient Confederate remount system contributed considerably to Early's cavalry woes. Southern cavalrymen supplied their own animals. If a horse died in service, the Confederate government paid the creature's appraised worth in badly inflated currency, but the dismounted trooper faced the chore of finding a new ride on his own. As the war progressed, that task passed beyond difficulty to the level of near impossibility. The appraisal system documents an average 1861 value for cavalry mounts of $150. Two years later, with the war only half over, twice that much money was required just to board a horse for one month in Richmond. As the demands of an all-encompassing war made horseflesh valuable beyond measure, cavalrymen quickly learned that risking their private stock in battle made no sense. Personal courage aside, the nagging voice of common sense suggested that combat élan risked the horse and threatened to end the soldier's cavalry career. The same situation encouraged and stimulated emphasis on capturing horses and carrying them away from danger. That aspect of Confederate cavalry affairs figured prominently in the closing phases of the first battle of Winchester on May 25, 1862. Two years later, operations in the Valley suffered dramatically from the same problem.

Most of the cavalrymen with Early's army in the Valley in 1864 suffered also from the fact that their homes were situated behind enemy lines. Many of them came from counties that belonged to the newly proclaimed Unionist state of West Virginia. Others lived in areas of the Valley itself and in south-western Virginia where Federal columns were running amok, armed not only with muskets and commissary requisition forms, but also with flaming torches. The effect of such circumstances on mounted men with the means to ride home can readily be imagined. Few other American fighting men in the nation's long history have faced the ordeal of standing to fight in a distant place while their homefolks had to cope with destruction and want at the hands of a hostile invading force. Cavalry units from other parts of Virginia and the South that were considered to be more stalwart included relatively few men whose homes lay at the mercy of an enemy; infantry from the subjugated counties had far less mobility to employ in heading for home. The mobility of mounted men lent wings to intentions probably shared by many envious soldiers of the other arms.

The officers who attempted to lead the Valley cavalry almost invariably recognized the existence of serious shortcomings in both men and units. The more sympathetic observers offered explanations and qualifiers, but even they virtually never pretended to deny the problems. Colonel Thomas T. Munford, who came from the "regular" cavalry service east of the mountains, explained that the Valley mounted units "were armed with miserable guns for the service exacted of them, and . . . never had a fair show . . . [and] could not do impossibilities." General John McCausland described his horsemen as "mostly western Virginia boys who had formed their local militia companies and joined up with us. They had the makings of fine soldiers—none better. But they were undisciplined."

McCausland was among those charged with instilling that requisite discipline. A story told about the general illustrates the independence traditional with civilian soldiers and especially pronounced in the Valley ranks. A private ordered to report to McCausland with an ax for fatigue duty in camp examined the task that his superior pointed out to him with some care. "Can *one man* do it?" inquired the reluctant lumberjack. McCausland assured him that one man could. "Well, then," said the detail, shouldering his ax, "I'll go back to camp," leaving McCausland bemused in his wake.

General Basil W. Duke of Kentucky, who had some experience with cavalry operations in Virginia's secondary theaters, wrote a long and thoughtful description of the late-war plight of the irregular cavalryman:

> Almost destitute of hope that the cause for which he fought would triumph, and fighting on from instinctive obstinate pride . . . is it surprising that he became wild and lawless, that he adopted a rude creed in which strict conformity to military regulations and a nice obedience to general orders held not very prominent places? This condition obtained in a far greater degree with the cavalry employed in the "outpost" departments than with the infantry or the soldiery of the large armies. . . . Many Confederate cavalry men so situated left their commands altogether and became guerrillas, salving their consciences with the thought that the desertion was not to the enemy.

Duke's apologia is notable not only for its sympathetic perspective, but also for its calm acceptance of the basic fact that irregular cavalry suffered from shortcomings so pervasive as to be routine.

Marylander Bradley T. Johnson expressed mixed admiration and dismay over the Valley cavalry he commanded in 1864. He described his brigade as "about eight hundred half-armed and badly disciplined mountaineers from southwest Virginia, who would fight like veterans when they pleased, but had no idea of permitting their own sweet wills to be controlled by any orders, no matter from whom emanating." Johnson used three adjectives to describe his men that nicely define the situation: they were, he wrote, "brave . . . fearless . . . [and] un-disciplined." General W. H. F. Payne saw more thorns than roses in the mixture. Of his own command, Payne wrote, "The discipline of the Brigade is not near so good as it ought to be." He suggested—in vain, of course—that cumbersome court-martial procedures be streamlined in order to make discipline rapid and visible. Another Confederate officer wrote in similar spirit soon after the campaign that "want of discipline had greatly demoralized the men."

When the Valley cavalry moved into northern North Carolina during one winter in search of forage for both man and beast, their demeanor quickly prompted outraged cries for relief from local civilians. In response to one cavalry officer's half-hearted attempts to deny the reports, Governor Zebulon B. Vance wrote to the secretary of war: "The concurrent testimony of the cit-izens of about twenty counties with at least fifty letters to that effect in my office would seem to be sufficient to establish a fact of general notoriety." During October 1864, at the height of Early's campaign in the Valley, Secretary of War James A. Seddon complained bitterly about the "most predatory and dis-creditable manner" in which supposedly friendly cavalry had "plundered and ravaged without discrimination or hindrance, often inflicting most serious losses on the families of men in the Confederate Army or now in Yankee prisons." To Seddon's understandable horror, "even women are said to have been plundered." The secretary's plaintive conclusion echoed the forlorn hope of everyone connected with the problem: "Some decisive means seems necessary to restrain the license of our own irregular cavalry, and bring them into subordination and efficiency."

Drinking contributed to the disarray in the Valley cavalry. An officer who led some of Early's mounted men to the out-skirts of Washington in July 1864 responded to a question about why the command halted before penetrating into the streets of the Federal capital city. In the words of an infantry-man listening to the conversation, "He replied he was afraid if he ever got his men into town he would never get them out. . . . They would have filled up the bar rooms and saloons and that would have been the last of them." A member of the 14th Virginia Cavalry wrote late in 1864 in his diary: "It was a drunken spree. There has been a real Regimental drunk today." A few weeks later he noted, "There are few who don't indulge. I am sorry to see it."

In July, a member of the staff of General John C. Breckinridge added his vote to the worried official chorus when he wrote of Early's "wild cavalry," about "the inefficiency of which there was constant complaint and almost daily exhibition." When word reached Richmond during August of renewed cavalry problems in the Valley, General Braxton Bragg hurried a note to Early in solicitous language that did nothing to challenge Bragg's reputation as a master of equivocation. In endeavoring to rein in and reorganize the wild cavalry, Bragg suggested, Early should do something, but not too much. "It is feared that too radical a change may produce dissatisfaction in those commands raised mostly in the country now held by the enemy and cause many desertions," the Richmond bureaucrat declared. "At the same time it is felt that some stringent measures are necessary to secure discipline and prevent disaster." Early must have snarled when he read that fence-straddling exhortation, but in fact it presented nothing more than a truth already well known to everyone in a position of responsibility in the Valley.

Early's frank and earnest correspondence with R. E. Lee reviewed the options for revising the structure of his cavalry, without any need for Bragg's restatement of the patently obvious. The tactical verities militated against success for his horsemen, Early knew. Their equipment—with rifles, rather than pistols and carbines, and without sabres—left the cavalrymen unable to fight mounted, and they did not like to fight afoot. In either position, efforts to use the men came up firmly against the fact that "the command is and has been demoralized all the time." An obvious and much-mooted solution was to attach the men to infantry commands. Early liked the idea, but feared it would not work. "It would be better if they could all be put into the infantry," the Valley commander told Lee, "but, if that were tried, I am afraid they would all run off."

Brigadier General Bradley Tyler Johnson

Early continued to squirm on the horns of that unforgiving di-
lemma throughout the 1864 Valley campaign.

Perhaps the most telling indictment against the undisciplined Valley cavalry came in an official document submitted
by General Bradley T. Johnson in August. In reporting on operations early in that month, Johnson chronicled a degree of
misbehavior almost beyond fathoming. "Every crime in the

catalogue of infamy has been committed," Johnson declared, most of it perpetrated upon Southerners and the families of Confederate soldiers.

Highway robbery of watches and pocket-books was of ordinary occurrence: the taking of breast-pins, finger-rings, and earrings frequently happened. Pillage and sack of private dwellings took place hourly. A soldier of an advance guard robbed of his gold watch the Catholic clergyman of Hancock on his way from church on Sunday . . . in the public streets. Another of a rear guard nearly brained a private of Company B, First Maryland Cavalry, for trying to prevent his sacking a woman's trunk and stealing her clothes and jewels. A lieutenant at Hancock exacted and received $1,000 . . . of a citizen; a soldier packed up a woman's and a child's clothing, which he had stolen in the presence of the highest officials, unrebuked. . . . Ransoms varied from $750 to $150, according to the size of habitation. . . . A lieutenant knocked down and kicked an aged woman who has two sons in the Confederate army, and after choking the sister locked her in a stable and set fire to it. This was because the two women would not give up horses he and his fellow thieves wished to steal.

The general concluded his ghastly report (from which the passage above is only an extract) with a bit of arrantly misplaced optimism when he suggested that some means might be found to inculcate "a higher tone of morals and discipline" in every Southern soldier "which will restrain him from disgracing himself and his countrymen by such deeds." The inevitable excesses of individuals in war aside, it is impossible to envision any large group of cavalry from the Army of Northern Virginia behaving in like fashion. Jubal Early's horror at the prospect of solving his cavalry needs with such a crew of highwaymen can readily be imagined, and perhaps understood, under the impact of evidence such as that presented by Johnson.

The deficiencies of the cavalry organizations and their constituent members make strikingly clear the importance of

solid leadership. The lack of discipline early in the war made
the task of later officers all but impossible. Any analysis of
Valley cavalry leaders must begin with Turner Ashby, who
shone brightly in the war's early days in that region and who
remained in death the *beau sabreur* for a whole generation of
Valley youth. Viewed in a larger military context, Ashby deserves laurels as perhaps the finest company commander of
cavalry in American military history. At levels above that,
however—and he rose through four ranks beyond captain—
Ashby progressed steadily further out of his depth. The gaggle
of mounted youngsters trailing in his wake in early 1862
would and could do anything he asked. Ashby eventually commanded twenty-seven companies unorganized into battalions
or regiments, and at least twenty-six of them operated below
par at any given time because they were beyond the reach of
his personal magnetism. General Richard Taylor deftly summarized Ashby's strength and his great weakness, and at the
same time identified the role of a discipline that the Valley
cavalry never would know. Ashby was, Taylor wrote,

> the most daring and accomplished rider in a region of horse-
> men. His courage was so brilliant as to elicit applause from
> friend and foe, but he was without capacity or disposition to
> enforce discipline on his men. I witnessed his deep chagrin at
> the conduct of our troopers after the enemy had been driven
> from Winchester in May. With proper organization and disci-
> pline, his bold riders under his lead might have accomplished all
> that [was possible] . . . for light cavalry. . . . Valor is as necessary
> now as ever in war, but disciplined, subordinated valor, admit-
> ting the courage and energies of all to be welded and directed to
> a common end.

Ashby was the archetype against which the Valley cavalry
measured all of his successors, without knowing that the yard-
stick was itself out of plumb.

During the early stages of the 1864 Valley campaign, a ster-
ling but largely unheralded cavalry officer held the potential to
lead the motley crew of horsemen there in the right direction. Brigadier General William E. Jones carried the *nom de*

guerre "Grumble," which he had earned fairly and well in a succession of clashes that displayed an unlovely temperament. General J. E. B. Stuart and "Grumble" Jones thoroughly loathed one another, but Jones had given indications that he was nearly as skillful in military affairs as he was maladroit in human affairs. Unfortunately, on June 5, 1864, with the campaign almost a month old, Jones fell victim to the criminal indolence of two subordinates at the disastrous battle of Piedmont. A Federal bullet struck him down after cavalry generals John C. Vaughn and John D. Imboden stolidly watched the enemy advance unhindered across their front at the crisis of the battle. In this fashion one of the brightest hopes for leadership for the Valley cavalry fell dead, having been put to death by that very same inept Valley cavalry as thoroughly as though by guillotine.

Two months and two days after the debacle at Piedmont, Generals John McCausland and Bradley T. Johnson collaborated on a mutual embarrassment at Moorefield that has received far less attention than it deserves. Between them, McCausland and Johnson distributed their troops in a manner so slovenly that they were surprised and routed in what must be adjudged the most thorough fiasco suffered by any Confederate cavalry force in the Virginia theater during the entire war.

Into this unsettled picture rode Major General Fitzhugh Lee, a seasoned and successful divisional commander from the more regular cavalry units east of the mountains and a man of solid reputation. No better man for the job could be imagined. Fitz Lee's uncle, General R. E. Lee, and Jubal Early both must have expected great things from the young officer. Whether their expectations would have been fulfilled must remain a matter for conjecture, because a bullet slammed into Fitz Lee's thigh during his first real action in the Valley, at the Third Battle of Winchester. Its effects put young Lee out of service throughout the campaign. In ill omen, enemy fire also killed Lee's mare, Nelly Gray, who had served him well since 1861 under all manner of enemy attention.

Eight general officers who struggled with cavalry command in the 1864 Valley deserve a summary review in order to grasp the scope of Early's resources. W. H. F. Payne attended Virginia Military Institute, practiced law, and was thirty-four years old at the height of the campaign. John C. Vaughn was an uneducated Tennessee merchant, aged forty. Bradley T. Johnson was a thirty-five-year-old Maryland lawyer, educated at Princeton. William L. Jackson, aged thirty-nine and another lawyer, was a second cousin to the infinitely more distinguished Thomas J. Jackson. John D. Imboden, aged forty-one, practiced law after an education at Washington College in Lexington. John McCausland graduated from VMI and taught there before the war; he was only twenty-eight during the 1864 Valley campaign. Lunsford Lindsay Lomax was also twenty-eight and a Virginian, educated at the U.S. Military Academy. Williams C. Wickham was a forty-four-year-old lawyer, educated at the University of Virginia.

A composite drawn from that group would be a lawyer slightly older than thirty-five years, with little or no military experience. Training at Virginia Military Institute helped to prepare Payne and McCausland for their tasks, but only West Point educated L. L. Lomax actually had antebellum experience as a military officer. Of the eight, only Wickham and Lomax had held responsible commands in "regular" Confederate cavalry service. It probably was more than coincidence that Wickham and Lomax also proved to be the most solid officers, though neither won any notable laurels in the Valley. The other six, to one degree or another, simply were not up to their assigned tasks. Perhaps those tasks were more than could reasonably have been asked of anyone.

Imboden remains more familiar today to students of the war than many others of like rank and service because of the proverbial relative strengths of the pen and the sword. His writings, in the familiar *Battles and Leaders* set among other forums, understandably throw favorable light on his accomplishments. In some instances Imboden found an opportunity to elbow his way into the reflected glow of the legendary "Stonewall" Jackson. During the 1864 operations, however, many superiors and colleagues held Imboden up as the symbol of Valley cavalry incompetence. General John C. Breckinridge telegraphed to Richmond in June: "The cavalry under Imboden

Brigadier General Williams Carter Wickham

doing less than nothing. If a good general officer cannot be sent for them at once they will go to ruin." When the cavalry flank at the Third Battle of Winchester collapsed, a Confederate staff officer identified the fastest of the fleeing men (whether rightly or wrongly) as from Imboden's command. "When a number of Imboden's Cavalry rushed pell mell through the streets of Winchester, far in advance of all other fugitives from the battle-field," this witness testified, "a large number of the most respectable ladies joined hands & formed a line across the principal street, telling the cowardly Cavalrymen that they should not go any further unless they ran their horses over their bodies."

Brigadier General John Daniel Imboden

Bradley T. Johnson, himself outspoken on the lack of discipline, stuck others as part of the problem. After the disaster at Moorefield, Jedediah Hotchkiss of Early's staff wrote home to his wife and described Johnson as "culpably negligent" and the affair as "extremely disgraceful." "There is but one opinion about Johnson," Hotchkiss said pointedly, "and the only wish is that he had been captured also. He . . . is a bold & dashing fellow, but has no discipline."

Reports of John C. Vaughn's abysmal misbehavior at Piedmont attained such wide circulation that Jubal Early probably was not surprised to find Vaughn incompetent. Within hours after Early reached Lynchburg, he sent a panicked telegram back to Richmond. "It is of the utmost importance to have another commander than [Vaughn]," wrote the crisis-beset lieutenant general. "Answer at once."

The field-grade officers of the Valley cavalry doubtless varied as much as would any other cross section of humanity, when elected by those intended for command; but there is little evidence that any men of high potential were waiting to fill the widening command breach. One Valley regiment (the 17th Virginia Cavalry) began the war with a colonel described as "a good hearted man but not much for emergencies," and also as "a very cautious man . . . anxious that no one should get hurt and more especially himself." To that same regiment belonged a major who sought to return to command during the 1864 Valley campaign, despite having misappropriated more than a thousand dollars to his own use earlier in the war by filing pay vouchers for nonexistent men and forging approval signatures on the documents. Some of the wildcat cavalry in the theater probably would have admired his imagination and style, but there seems little reason to believe that the embezzler could offer much of use to the faltering Confederate cause.

Some observers suggested the obvious expedient of combining the irresolute units with better-disciplined organizations that had been imported from Lee's army to reinforce Early. General Robert Ransom, who had struggled with the Valley cavalry problem earlier in the year before being transferred, wrote a very long proposal that shuffled units all around the organizational chart. To deal with Vaughn's brigade, Ransom suggested, "Dismount at once the whole of it." Some of Imboden's units might be combined and then transferred intact into Wickham's regular brigade, "at the same time relieving Brigadier-General Imboden." The stray battalions, operating as permanently frail regiments, should be consolidated into genuine regimental organizations to be led by "meritorious officers from the cavalry of Northern Virginia." In that manner the men "will be taught to fight; and the indifferent officers gotten rid of." Ransom also suggested that "there should be at least three inspectors at each division headquarters." Ransom's thoughtful proposals, and others like them, foundered on the twin shoals of bureaucratic indifference and hostility to change among the independent and disdainful units that were their targets.

Thomas Lafayette Rosser went to his grave convinced that he was the "Saviour of the Valley," as some hopeful and incautious journalists styled him during the early fall of 1864. Rosser's advent in the Valley raised hopes that he would indeed be its savior at a time when miracles clearly were needed. He was the last of the fresh hopes for the Valley cavalry, and arrived just as the final chapter in the 1864 campaign opened.

Tom Rosser was born in Virginia but had resided in Texas since his early youth. Five days after his natal state seceded, and two weeks before he was due to graduate, young Rosser resigned from West Point and offered his services to the Confederacy. By the time of the Battle of Cedar Creek, the general was twenty-eight years old. Despite an enormous cache of Rosser manuscripts at the University of Virginia, no scholarly biography of the energetic but enigmatic man yet exists. The surviving letters reveal an enthusiastic man-child of mercurial bent, writing to a young wife in moods belligerent and pious and various other shades as well. Rosser labored under a deep suspicion of "Jeb" Stuart, whom he thought—without any justification—did not support him in his breathless quest for promotion. The young man's letters to his wife often speak harshly of his superior in terms and on subjects that should

Brigadier General Thomas Lafayette Rosser

interest Stuart biographers. They also show Rosser as queru-
lous, complaining, and generally unlovely. Long after Stuart's
death deprived him of that target, Rosser carried on an ardent

quarrel with his wartime rival, Colonel T. T. Munford. Their postbellum paper feud, which survives in gratifying volume, is amusing, entertaining, and informative by turns.

The huge and athletic frame of Rosser contained a warrior's spirit that marked him as a leader of men in mounted battle. His vast store of personal bravery prompted otherwise unimpressed witnesses to use phrases such as "Brave as a Lion" about Rosser. Rather like Turner Ashby, though, Rosser's grasp apparently did not extend beyond the reach of his eye and his sword arm.

In May 1864, a young officer in the 35th Virginia Cavalry Battalion ("the Comanches"), of Rosser's famous Laurel Brigade, concisely reported his dashed hopes that Rosser would prove to be a capable leader. "We have fought hard and faithfully and lost heavily," wrote Captain Franklin M. Myers, "but I can't see why we should have done so. My bright dream that Rosser was one of the first calvery Generals in our service is gone. He is no General at all." Myers praised Rosser's bravery in the same line that he damned his judgment: "As brave a man as ever drew breath, but knows no more about putting a command into a fight than a school boy." Deterioration of morale and efficiency in the Laurel Brigade followed with dreadful certainty. "We have lost confidence in him so fast that he can't get a good fight out of us any more," stated Myers, "unless we know positively what we are fighting."

Given his observations on Rosser the brigade commander, Myers cannot have harbored many illusions about the general's prospects in even more complex and responsible roles. Other Confederates great and small echoed Myers's judgment after Rosser failed in the Valley. Virginian Mark T. Alexander wrote from Rosser's camp in the fall that, sycophants aside, the general "is extremely unpopular with the Division, they having been whipped in every fight since he has been with us, they say by his bad management." The coterie around headquarters, Alexander thought, were "a set of men who would black his boots if necessary." The rest of the mounted Southerners in the Valley longed for a rapid convalescence for Fitzhugh Lee and his prompt return to command.

After the war, Early's dissatisfaction with Rosser bubbled over in one of those newspaper brawls that so attracted Early and that prompted him gleefully to dip his pen in vitriol. The "somewhat notorious" Rosser, Early declared, had, in describing events in the Valley, "shown his utter disregard for the truth." One of Rosser's published sallies prompted his former commander to write of the cavalryman: "Having previously figured extensively as a falsifier of history, he has recently appeared in another role—that of a consummate ass, and it must be confessed that he has proved himself an adept in that character." Warming to his task, Early eventually compared Rosser's apostasy from the truth to that of Judas Iscariot, concluding that Christ's betrayer had much the better of the comparison: Judas, after all, finally threw away his blood money and hanged himself. Were Rosser to emulate that example, Early suggested, "we might regard the act as some atonement for [his] apostasy and the most creditable act [he] could now perform."

Jubal Early the postwar controversialist was not necessarily the same man struggling with harsh realities in the fall of 1864, but neither did his loathing for Tom Rosser in the 1880s spring whole from the ground. Early probably asked himself at the beginning of October 1864 the same question his army eagerly considered: Is Rosser as good as we hope he is and as good as he sometimes has looked? Is he another Grumble Jones or Fitz Lee? Or is Rosser another out of the Imboden/Vaughn mold? The answers would bring comfort only to men in blue in 1864. At the time, Early probably watched the results with more sorrow than venom, but what he saw did supply ample grist for his subsequent written squabbles with Rosser.

In a lively postscript to the campaign, played out in 1887, Tom Rosser found another opportunity to cast himself as the "Saviour of the Valley." By then the ex-Confederate had gained considerable prominence through association with George A. Custer, his West Point friend and 1870s hunting companion on the plains. In 1887, Phil Sheridan announced, with all of his considerable insensitivity, that he planned to visit the

Shenandoah Valley to see whether it had yet recovered from his 1864 visit. Sheridan had trampled Southern spirits with impunity during Reconstruction, but a decade later his remarks raised a publicity firestorm. Rosser, who not coincidentally was essaying a run at Virginia politics just then, led the outcry that ensued. He had more success in that endeavor than he had against Sheridan in 1864, when denouements were determined by the possession of big and well-armed battalions.

The "regular" cavalry from east of the mountains that fought under Rosser in the Valley included some relatively new commanders whose performance is difficult to gauge. Williams C. Wickham seems to have performed solidly, with potential for good results given an opportunity, but he could not take hold against the racing ebb tide. During the fall Wickham went off to Richmond to occupy the seat he held in the Confederate States Congress. Lunsford Lindsay Lomax fell into the same category. He was well trained and apt, with successes to his credit in northern Virginia, but he arrived at his opportunities late in the war. The twenty-eight-year-old professional soldier had performed creditably in the thrashing of Sheridan at Trevilian Station in mid-June 1864, coming away with George Custer's mess chest and wagon, among other trophies. A few days later Lomax took out an advertisement in the *Richmond Examiner* enumerating the stolen Southern silverware in Custer's gear and offering its return to the lawful owners. Lomax's performance in the Valley seems in retrospect similar to that of Wickham—solid and apparently hopeful, but in fact hopeless. Had his chance at important command come early in the war, Lomax might today be part of the Confederate cavalier legend with an equestrian bronze reminder gracing some Virginia roadside.

That the poverty of cavalry command in the 1864 Valley operations would in many instances extend to field grade officers was inevitable. The immutable arithmetic of war had subtracted some of the best leaders by way of casualty lists. Others had been promoted out of regimental command— many of them to positions beyond their capacity, as we have seen. The famous 1st Virginia Cavalry will serve as a vivid case study. A succession of notable cavalrymen had com-

Major General Lunsford Lindsay Lomax

manded this regiment during the war, beginning with Jeb
Stuart himself. Later Fitz Lee was colonel of the regiment. So
was Grumble Jones. Colonel James Henry Drake followed

those able men. Although Drake never shared the fame of the
other three, his men loved and respected him. The forty-year-
old prewar plasterer, mechanic, and militia officer typified a
class of men who blossomed to competence under the demands of warfare. By late 1864, however, all of those men were
gone from the regiment; three of them were dead. That left
an aristocratic Virginian named Richard Welby Carter as colonel of the illustrious command, and Carter was an unmiti-
gated disaster.

Welby Carter had attended Virginia Military Institute, where
he doubtless learned—but apparently did not assimilate—that
school's meticulous code of behavior. The Institute files show
that young Carter encountered continuous disciplinary trouble
during his school days. At the end of the 1856 school year, he
stood next-to-last in his class in general merit, while leading
all of his peers in demerits despite having been absent—on
suspension for misconduct—during part of the term. Further
misdeeds a few weeks into the new session that summer led to
Carter's dismissal from the Institute.

Early in 1863, by now a Confederate lieutenant colonel,
Carter was victor in a bizarre and much-discussed love quad-
rangle that resulted in the suicide of a failed suitor. James
Keith Boswell of Stonewall Jackson's staff called Carter "a coward" and denounced him "about as vigorously as a good and
consistent christian . . . could well do." Another of Jackson's
staff officers called the cavalryman "white livered."

One of the colonel's troopers was even harsher in his judgment than were the staff officers. He wrote: "Carter, notwith-
standing he was always fat and looked greasy, I never knew of
any member of the regiment to possess enough of cannibalism
to ever wish to eat him." The same soldier reported what the
whole army soon came to know, that at Tom's Brook "our be-
loved Colonel Carter had run twenty five miles, never stop-
ping until he got inside our infantry line at New Market."
Expecting a reincarnation of Stuart, Lee, Jones, or Drake might
have been unreasonable, but a frantic race to the rear fell far
short of acceptable performance. A formal court martial soon
expressed that opinion and cashiered Colonel Carter.

Virginia's Governor William "Extra Billy" Smith attempted to intervene on Carter's behalf. The governor wrote to Jefferson Davis, in decidedly mid-nineteenth-century fashion, that he knew the Carter family well; that none of them could possibly be a coward; and that the family reputation must be protected. The president did not accept this line of reasoning. The unhappy war experience of the one-time colonel ended in a Northern prison where he was taken after being captured in February 1865 while hiding at his home. The Illinois officer who found Carter huddled behind an old chimney described him as "a large portly man in his drawers and stocking feet." The Northerner added with amazement that a black servant who had fled slavery and joined up with the captors identified Carter as his father. Carter's father later wrote to Federal authorities on his son's behalf, offering the irrefragable argument that the Confederate army had cashiered his son, so he was not a Confederate and not liable to imprisonment. The plight of the 1st Virginia Cavalry and the uncomfortable story of its late-war leader highlight in dark but unmistakable colors the state of Confederate mounted troops in 1864 in the Shenandoah Valley.

After examining the litany of horrors Early faced from both cavalry troops and cavalry leaders, the battlefield developments themselves hardly hold any major surprise. Repeatedly during the late summer and fall of 1864, Confederate cavalry fell victim to Federal mounted forces that outnumbered them by large proportions. In the process, momentum built for the Northern squadrons and drained away from their Southern counterparts. It is not a glaring exaggeration to suggest that when infantry forces clashed in the three largest battles of the campaign, Early's veterans fought with amazing fortitude against Sheridan's corps until their lines were compromised by collapse of their mounted colleagues on a flank.

At the Third Battle of Winchester on September 19, Gordon and Ramseur and Rodes stood stalwart against swarming Federals for hours, and Rodes died in the process. They blistered each Federal infantry effort and inflicted thousands of casualties (although Sheridan finally won the field, he lost in one day more men than Stonewall Jackson killed and wounded during the course of his entire fabled 1862 campaign in this same Valley). It is hard to imagine how any infantry could have done more than Early's achieved that day east of Winchester. In fact, few performances on other battlefields of the war equal it. The rupture on his left that doomed Early's army came through ground held primarily by his cavalry. Whether any available force could have held under the circumstances may be argued, but the familiar result left the Confederate army in rout. Significantly, most of the substantive rearguard efforts that can be discerned today, from accounts of that chaotic evening, came from infantry units. At Winchester and elsewhere in the Valley, the cavalry betrayed its ineptitude by failing to discharge its traditional screening function during retreats.

Three days after driving Early from Winchester, Sheridan closed with the Confederates again a few miles south of Strasburg at Fisher's Hill. The position there to which Early had retreated seemed to have enough natural strength to offer the Southerners a bulwark of some consequence. On its right (eastern) flank, Fisher's Hill—really a succession of hills perpendicular to the Valley Pike—dropped precipitously into the North Fork of the Shenandoah River. Across the front of Fisher's Hill, separating it from ground the Federals occupied before the battle, ran Tumbling Run. That stream lives up to its name by bubbling cheerfully through the fields on a twisting course. The run served as a moat of sorts below the Southern line, too small to pose a major military obstacle, but indicative of a deeply cut ravine that separated the armies. Northerners attacking across the run would have to descend to it under fire, then clamber up slopes so formidable as to be virtually impregnable if defended with even moderate strength.

The only weak point in Early's line lay on his left, and even that zone included some points useful for defense. The western wall of the Valley loomed there, as though designed for a line to anchor on, and while Fisher's Hill lost some of its elevation and regularity on the left, good ground nearby gave Early terrain advantages. The immense strength of the Confederate right must have been apparent to the most unlettered private soldier on either side (though Sheridan's first plan was to attack there, before wiser heads prevailed). By the same token the need for Confederate caution on Early's left was strikingly apparent.

In what must be adjudged an egregious tactical blunder, perhaps his largest of the long campaign, Early packed his seasoned infantry into the powerful position on his right and scattered his unreliable cavalry out on the more sensitive left. The only faint mitigation that might be offered for Early's dreadful misjudgment is the fact that the Valley Pike ran through his right. To have his line broken atop that crucial artery would have constituted a marginally greater disaster than a rupture on the left. It seems certain, however, that neither end needed to face destruction had Early distributed his forces rationally.

On the afternoon of September 22, Early reaped the bitter fruits of his faulty alignment. Federals under George Crook moved up the mountainside, then south beyond the Southern flank, then roared down the slope and shattered the Confederate cavalry along Early's left. It is, of course, impossible to say precisely what would have happened had veteran Confederate infantry stood in the way. What is of record is that the horsemen ordered to hold that ground dissolved in record time. The Confederate cavalry had too few numbers and, more important, neither the spirit nor the efficiency to repulse or even impede Crook's assault.

The scampering cavalrymen disgusted, though did not surprise, their infantry mates on up the line. After the war, one of the foot soldiers recorded with undisguised disdain the demeanor of the first straggler who dashed past: "After a slight fire on the left a cavalryman came down our line telling the men they were flanked. This did much for Sheridan and that fellow should have a [Yankee] pension. I have often regretted I did not shoot him and shall always regret not having arrested him. It might have saved us from a disgraceful defeat. It certainly would have been stopped further to our left. He passed over three-fourths of our line telling every man 'we are flanked' and 'the enemy is behind us.' "

The vacuum on the left quickly unraveled Early's line, and his men fled in complete rout up the Valley, replicating in remarkable detail their unhappy experience three days earlier. A North Carolina infantry officer described the weary loathing with which his colleagues viewed their cavalry detachment and recounted an episode that nicely encapsulated that feeling. "The Confederate foot soldier was not noted for his admiration or his respect for his compatriot who bestrode a horse," the Carolinian wrote. Furthermore, "Early's foot soldiers' love for a cavalryman was even below the Confederate average." To the infantry, the mounted men in the Valley seemed to dash "hither and thither with no object apparent to prejudiced eyes, except that of keeping as much space as possible between themselves and the foe."

During the frightful ordeal of racing away from Fisher's Hill, the Carolinian officer passed a Confederate who had composed a ditty in tribute to the shortcomings of the Valley cavalry. "For some cause known only to their whimsical philosophy," the foot soldiers held Imboden's cavalry as "an especial object of their disesteem. By way of derision they called it 'Jimboden's' cavalry." The embittered lyricist near Fisher's Hill aimed his song at "Jimboden," though in fact the cavalry at fault on that day had been under L. L. Lomax. As the North Carolinian rode southward amidst the discouraged mass, he noticed,

> close beside the road along which the troops poured in confusion, a ragged, dejected, unkempt "Confed" crouched over a little fire, regarding naught, absorbed alone in warming numbed fingers and toes, for the day was chilly. As he crouched and shivered he droned a song in whose tone disgust, despair and disdain all strove for the mastery. The song, which must have been rich, was lost except the following stanzas caught as a group of officers rode by:
> "Old Jimboden's gone up the spout,
> And Old Jube Early's about played out."

A few weeks later "Old Jube" Early proved to the astonishment of many on both sides that he was not played out. Precisely one month after the disaster at the Third Battle of Winchester, Early was back at Sheridan's throat and close to destroying him north of Strasburg. Before he completed his metamorphosis, though, Early faced the misfortune of picking up the pieces after yet another cavalry debacle.

The cavalry embarrassment at Tom's Brook on October 9 had its roots in the savage destruction of much of the Valley's substance under Sheridan's orders. As Northern troopers moved down the Valley in early October, they methodically destroyed everything in their path. Tom Rosser did not need to prod his Southern horsemen after the burners; many of the pursuing riders saw their own homes and families brutalized during those terrible days. Some Federal detachments with arson on their minds ran into Confederate parties who butchered them as part of a new sort of war even uglier than the old variety. On a larger scale, though, the Confederate mounted units suffered a marked disaster when their outraged ardor led them too far from infantry support in desperate pursuit of vengeance.

When Rosser and Lomax came under heavy attack just south of Tom's Brook on October 9, their troopers stood and fought against enormous odds for some time. In the end, they succumbed and raced south up the Valley in abject rout. Rosser's own Laurel Brigade scattered no more widely or rapidly than any of the others, but its proud reputation and distinctive name prompted Early to pick on it in the aftermath. In a bitter (and botanically inaccurate) aside, Early cracked that "laurel is a running vine." Had the army commander been present, he would have greatly enjoyed another episode in the aftermath of Tom's Brook. As the rout slowed in exhaustion, Tom Rosser spied a regimental fragment carrying one of the unique Laurel Brigade flags. The general turned to Lomax and exclaimed with vestigial pride, "You see the Laurel Brigade brings out its flags." As the weary riders drew closer, Lomax said, "If I am not mistaken, that is one of my regiments coming out." Lomax was right. His men had either recaptured the laurel flag from the enemy or, more likely, had salvaged it from abandonment.

Jubal Early's greatest success in the campaign came on October 19 at Cedar Creek. As had happened twice before within a month, Early's army won the first three-fourths of a battle despite the odds against it. The opening success at Cedar Creek ran farther and deeper than at Winchester or Fisher's Hill, and in fact was equal to anything done by the Army of Northern Virginia in its storied campaigns of the war's middle phase. Almost all of the Confederate success on October 19 sprang, once again, from strong infantry performances. While John B. Gordon, Stephen Dodson Ramseur, and Joseph B. Kershaw drove three Federal corps from their positions, Early's cavalry accomplished almost nothing. Old Jube himself deserved half of the blame, because he sent about one-half of his available mounted force off to his right under Lomax on an ill-defined and hopeless mission. Having dissipated a large part of his already-inadequate cavalry strength by executive fiat, Early could only hope for results from Rosser's men and a few other tiny detachments.

Rosser and his force spent October 19 where Early habitually posted his cavalry—on the army's far left. In that zone Rosser virtually disappeared during the course of the day. Federal cavalry responsible for keeping him in check gradually recognized the absence of threat and eventually most of them went off to take part in fighting to the east. When Sheridan retrieved his fortunes late in the afternoon, Federal cavalry roared across the Confederate left, as at Winchester and Fisher's Hill. Giddy victory on the morning of October 19 transmogrified into defeat of the most total scope by nightfall. Attempts to hold back the triumphant Federals and to salvage something from the chaos fell yet again to a rear guard composed of infantry, not cavalry. The formula for disaster, vintage 1864 Valley, applied yet again at Cedar Creek.

Early's disorganized retreat from Cedar Creek marked the end of serious infantry fighting in the Valley. There remained still another cavalry failure that fall, as the Confederate horsemen drained the last bitter dregs from a cupful of defeats. On November 12 while infantry skirmished in desultory fashion, Rosser and Payne fought Northern cavalry with some success near Strasburg. At the same time around Nineveh, north of

Front Royal on ground that had been the scene of Stonewall
Jackson's triumphal affairs on May 23–24, 1862, McCausland
repulsed two attacks and concluded that he had finished a
good day's work. As his men nonchalantly ate dinner and fed
their horses, ignoring as usual the basic disciplinary and security measures necessary in disputed country, a renewed Federal
surge caught and destroyed them.

Early responded to this latest debacle by publishing names of
cowards in a written special order. The poltroons were to be
"transferred from Cavalry to Infantry, for misbehavior before
the enemy on Nov. 12th 1864." They also were to forfeit their
mounts—a serious punishment because the horses were private property and at that stage of the war carried a value almost as great as their weight in depreciated Confederate
currency. The fuming general doubtless found some catharsis
in being able to pinpoint even in a small way his frustrations
with the cavalry that had caused him so much grief. As the
fall of 1864 ended, though, anything that Jubal Early might
attempt to do with his frail cavalry arm was far too little and
far too late.

The question remains whether there ever was a time at
which Early could have straightened out the Valley cavalry,
or a means that could have achieved that end. During 1864,
the more regular cavalry supporting the Army of Northern
Virginia east of the mountains faced odds and disadvantages
not unlike those that overwhelmed Early's troopers. Lee's horsemen performed their assigned tasks and maintained a pre-
carious equilibrium. They contained hostile raids, scouted
advances, and screened retreats. Despite the loss of Stuart,
they deflected Sheridan's Richmond raid in May, and in early
June they thoroughly bludgeoned that officer's force during its
threat to the railroads in the Battle of Trevilian Station. The
era of rides around the Army of the Potomac was long gone by
the summer and fall of 1864, but dedicated and disciplined cavalry continued to play its assigned role for Lee at the time that
Early languished without effective mounted support.

Early's own infantry and its leaders also offered an abrupt
contrast to the demeanor of the Valley cavalry. Rodes, Gordon,
Ramseur, John Pegram, and Kershaw each displayed steady

competence and often brilliance. Their men performed in like manner, in the healthy positive spiral that results from good leadership nurturing good support, and vice versa.

By contrast, not one officer amongst Rosser, McCausland, Vaughn, Imboden, W. L. Jackson, B. T. Johnson, and Payne offered assets nearly as good as the worst of those infantry leaders. We owe it to those men to consider the salient question, Could anyone have done the job? The answer must be, probably not. Those cavalry leaders most susceptible to criticism for problems during Early's campaign were the ones who had been in their roles for a long time, and therefore had contributed to the lack of discipline and the ineptitude of troops and units that fell apart under the demands of that difficult period.

The irregular Valley cavalry, by its nature, required especially strong leadership, but more often than not it had done without that important guidance throughout the war. The circumstances of Early's 1864 Valley campaign redoubled the demand for strong leaders. Time and again the events of the campaign resulted in a requirement that the cavalry do near-impossibilities at moments of decision. In consequence, the poor caliber of the men and units was exposed under an unblinking spotlight, and the shortcomings of their leadership were magnified manifold. To compound and redouble this unhappy mix, General Early for his part was maladroit in his desperate attempts to make the best of a bad deal.

"I Resolved to Play a Bold Game"
John S. Mosby as a Factor
in the 1864 Valley Campaign

DENNIS E. FRYE

The Federal supply train made a perfect target as it moved through a shallow hollow just north of Berryville, Virginia. Canvas-covered wagons damp with morning dew glistened brightly as the sun edged over the crest of the Blue Ridge. Patches of fog hung over the column as it proceeded peacefully through the green pastures of early August. Dozens of wagons, hundreds of mules and horses, and a herd of fattened cattle stretched toward a misty northern horizon. Unknown to the escort of Union infantrymen, Confederate Lieutenant Colonel John Singleton Mosby and part of his Forty-third Battalion of Virginia Cavalry waited behind a ridgeline just one hundred yards east of the turnpike.

Suddenly a howitzer shell screeched through the fog and exploded near the train. Then a second missile smashed into the wagons, and the whole train "stopped and writhed in its centre as if a wound had been opened in its vitals." From the ridgetop rose three hundred ghostly shadows, materializing in seconds into charging, screaming, and shooting Rebel raiders. Pandemonium erupted as Union infantrymen stampeded in every direction, panicked by their misfortune. Horses and mules neighed and brayed and galloped in circles of confusion. Drivers snapped snakewhips, wheeling forward and backward, crashing teams madly into each other. Flames and smoke clouds soon brightened the sky as the partisans, with plunder and prisoners, evaporated into dawn's thin light. Twisted, smoldering wreckage remained behind, the calling card of John S. Mosby and his welcome to the new Valley commander— Philip H. Sheridan.

During the late summer and fall of 1864, Sheridan and Mosby coexisted uneasily in the military theaters of Northern Virginia and the lower Shenandoah Valley. Each man detested the other's brand of warfare, and both later embellished their campaigns to enhance their postwar reputations. Sheridan, for example, admitted in his *Memoirs* that his army outnumbered that of Jubal A. Early, but claimed his forces only equalled Early's on the battlefield because Mosby compelled him to maintain heavy detachments in his rear. "Sheridan was a great liar," Mosby once confided, "but gave us full credit for the trouble we gave him." An article written by Mosby in 1895 for the *Richmond Times* boldly asserted that his operations in the Valley and on the Manassas Gap Railroad "prevented Sheridan's cooperation with Grant and saved Richmond six months." Such hyperbole and self-aggrandizement by both antagonists, coupled with the clouded memories of veterans writing after the war, distort the actual situation in the late summer and fall of 1864. Sheridan conceded that guerrillas gave him "great annoyance"; but in terms of influencing the Valley campaign, what *real* impact did Mosby have upon Sheridan?

It is beyond dispute that Mosby was a hero in the South and a celebrity in the North when Sheridan arrived in the Valley on August 6, 1864. Attacks by Mosby, followed by hunts for Mosby, escapes by Mosby, and rumors about Mosby had become thrilling stories on front pages for almost eighteen months. Each successive exploit colored the pen of the reporter and attracted the admiring interest of thousands of new readers. "The beings painted by war correspondents as Mosby's men were as purely ideal creations as Blue-Beard and Jack-the-Giant-Killer," Mosby later wrote. "Yet the tales told by them made a lasting impression just as the kissing of pilgrims has worn away stones."

Mosby's enormous popularity and success attracted eager recruits, including John Munson, a seventeen-year-old Richmond lad who had walked fifty miles to join the partisan's command. "To my mind Mosby was the ideal fighting man, from the tip of his plume to the rowel of his sabre," Munson affectionately

Lieutenant Colonel John Singleton Mosby

recalled. "Joan of Arc never felt the call to go to battle any stronger than I felt it to join Mosby." But disappointment, and downright disillusionment, greeted the youthful admirer when he first cast eyes upon the "Gray Ghost." "The visions of splendor and magnificence that had filled my mind were swept away," despaired Munson as he witnessed a small, wiry, and plainly attired Mosby. "The total absence of visible might, the lack of swagger, the quiet demeanor of the man, all contributed to my astonishment and chagrin. He did not even strut."

Yet Mosby had strutted—and strutted conspicuously—behind Federal lines since January 1863. Within two months of crossing north of the Rappahannock to harass the rear of Joseph Hooker's Army of the Potomac, Mosby had gobbled up pickets, frightened away cavalry regiments, destroyed a train, torn up the Orange & Alexandria Railroad, and captured a brigadier general. An admiring J. E. B. Stuart, Mosby's superior, scarcely could contain his enthusiasm, and upon reporting one of Mosby's successes to Robert E. Lee, Stuart heard the commanding general exclaim: "Hurrah for Mosby! I wish I had a hundred like him." Mosby had become a legend.

Federal authorities felt otherwise. One Union cavalry officer branded Mosby's men not heroes, but "a gang of outlaws, robbers, and cowardly murderers, who never fought in the open, but attacked trains from the bushes and in the dark." Time and again, Federal cavalry hunted Mosby in vain; time and again, the bluecoats returned with no prize. Frustration gnawed at Yankee pride, and anger and bitter resentment increased with each search for the elusive partisan.

What factors contributed to Mosby's success? Federal negligence and incompetence accounted for some of his good fortune, but most of Mosby's victories can be attributed to a well-conceived tactical doctrine practiced zealously by the guerrilla chieftain. The foremost trademark in Mosby's tactical book was always to charge, never to be charged. "It was a rule from which . . . I never departed," Mosby declared. Crediting Frederick the Great with the maxim never to stand and receive a charge but always to act on the offensive, Mosby utilized the dash down a farm lane, over a ridgeline, or from out of the woods to stun even the most vigilant enemy. The sudden screaming and shooting produced instant paralysis, and although the veteran opponent often recovered in just seconds, too much time already had elapsed. "[When] I saw them halt," Mosby mused, "I knew then that they had lost heart and were beaten." Disarmed through demoralization and surprise, the Federals often lost large numbers of prisoners at minimal cost to Mosby.

A brace of six-shooting Colt pistols comprised the second weapon in Mosby's tactical arsenal. Their rapid, concentrated firepower at close range in conjunction with the clamoring charge forced many Federals to choose between a bullet or prison. "Revolvers in the hands of Mosby's men," one ranger claimed, "were as effective in surprise engagements as a whole line of light ordnance." As for the primary cavalry weapon used during the first years of the war, the sabre, Mosby considered it an antique and "as useless against a skillfully handled revolver as the wooden swords of harlequins." Clumsy, noisy, and ineffective except at flesh-to-flesh range, sabres rarely accompanied Mosby's men on expeditions.

Night strikes formed a third component of Mosby's tactical plan. Darkness veiled his movements, protected his smaller numbers from larger bodies of preying Federals, and better insured surprise against the target. "If he could make a raid at midnight," John Munson declared, "it pleased him greatly, as he held that sleeping men are easy to surround, and that it required at least five minutes for an awakened soldier to get into shape to fight." No Union soldier in northern Virginia or the lower Shenandoah Valley, from general to private, could consider himself safe from Mosby once the sun disappeared. Paranoid pickets constantly sounded alarms, usually false ones, which kept dozens of camps and hundreds of soldiers uneasy throughout the night. These alarms proved "very annoying," a satisfied Mosby opined, "for no human being knows how sweet sleep is but a soldier." Mosby concluded that the fierce Federal hostility toward him was "more on account of the sleep I made them lose than the number we killed or captured."

Thorough scouting comprised another chapter in Mosby's tactical book. From points of rendezvous east of the Blue Ridge, less than a three-day ride would take his men to the lines of the enemy in almost any direction. "It was my habit to go myself," Mosby boasted, "to find some weak and exposed place in the enemy's lines." In addition to locating targets, Mosby also scouted his route of advance, method of attack, and avenue of escape. "Mosby was the fastest 'scouter' I ever knew," recalled one partisan, "and could cover a dozen objective points, over a course of fifty miles from sunset to sunrise." Mosby admitted his arduous daytime scouting and his presence during night attacks permitted little relaxation: "I rarely rested for more than one day at a time." The Blue Ridge Mountains constituted the final element in Mosby's treatise on guerrilla tactics. The gaps, ravines, hidden pathways, and tree-covered slopes of the Blue Ridge frightened Federal pursuers and insured Mosby's men, as one remembered, "our city of refuge, our citadel, our fortress." "Without its aid and protection," partisan George Baylor affirmed, "our career in this section would have been short."

Guiding Mosby's hit-and-run tactics was a dangerous, but not novel, strategy. "My purpose was to weaken the armies invading Virginia by harassing their rear," Mosby explained. "As a [supply] line is only as strong as its weakest point, it was necessary for it to be stronger than I was at every point, in order to resist my attacks." Mosby hoped that employment of this strategy would keep Federal troops off the main battlefields, thereby reducing superior Union numbers at the front. Proud of his knowledge of military history, Mosby often cited the famed French military theorist Jomini in defense of his strategy: "The irregular warfare of the Cossacks did more to destroy the French army on the expedition to Moscow than the elite regiments of the Russian guard."

Despite Mosby's strategy of harassment, and despite his well-publicized success with its execution, Ulysses S. Grant made no mention of Mosby in his first instruction to new Valley commander Philip H. Sheridan. Preoccupied with the recent embarrassment of Jubal Early's incursion to Washington in early July, Grant insisted that Sheridan "put himself south of the enemy and follow him to the death." Although Mosby had exhibited expertise in preying on the lines of an enemy moving south, Grant apparently discounted the Rebel raider as a trivial menace or irrelevant sideshow. Sheridan promptly executed Grant's mandate. On August 12, six days after his arrival in the Valley, the confident Irishman reached Cedar Creek, fifty miles southwest of his supply base at Harpers Ferry. On August 13, Mosby struck at Berryville, leaving Sheridan's wagons in ashes. Two days later, Sheridan commenced retreating down the Valley, his first thrust south a failure.

The attack at Berryville epitomized Mosby's devotion to one fact of military operations: "The line that connects an army with its base of supplies is the heel of Achilles—its most vital and vulnerable point." In order to exploit weaknesses in Federal lines of supply, Mosby enunciated a policy of "incessant attacks" designed to compel the enemy either to "greatly contract his lines or to reinforce them." He identified three specific objectives to carry out this goal: destroy supply trains; isolate an army from its base and individual corps from each other; and break up means of conveying intelligence and capture dispatches to confuse plans. The question requiring examination is this: Did Mosby successfully fulfill these objectives against Sheridan in his Valley campaign?

At first glance, the attack at Berryville suggests that Mosby forced Sheridan's retrograde from Cedar Creek nearly to Harpers Ferry. Partisan John Scott contends in his 1867 biography of Mosby that the exploit "compelled" Sheridan's retreat and required him to "subsist on short rations for a week." Ranger James J. Williamson, writing about Mosby's adventures thirty years after the war, declared Berryville "a severe blow" to Sheridan, who, "crippled by the loss of his supplies and fearful of another attack," hurriedly fell back to safer territory.

Such accounts examine the situation through a myopic Confederate lens. An exchange of dispatches between Grant and Sheridan reveals a decision to withdraw from Cedar Creek without regard to Mosby's attack. On August 12, the day previous to the Berryville strike, Grant's concern that Lee had dispatched reinforcements from Petersburg toward the Valley prompted instructions that Sheridan be "cautious and act now on the defensive." Sheridan received this message on the thirteenth, promptly informing Grant he had failed to get south of Early and that his Cedar Creek position "was a very bad one" for defensive purposes. The next day, Sheridan reaffirmed that the line at Cedar Creek "cannot be held" and announced his intention to withdraw to Winchester "at my leisure." On the fourteenth, Grant again urged Sheridan to "enjoin caution"; the following morning, "Little Phil" began a week-long retrograde to Halltown, considered by him the only defensible position in the lower Valley. Sheridan made no mention of Mosby's attack, other than to say the Rebel guerrilla had "burned six wagons." Mosby's strike at Berryville thus carried little weight when compared to Grant's warnings to be cautious and act on the defensive. Mosby certainly did not, as he later claimed, make Sheridan "run 50 miles."

Discrepancies in numbers present another interesting aspect of the Berryville wagon train episode. In his report to General Lee, Mosby claimed he destroyed seventy-five loaded wagons and captured more than two hundred beef cattle, two hundred prisoners, and five to six hundred horses and mules. Mosby further stated that his three hundred raiders routed the seven to eight hundred infantry guarding the train. By 1902, Joseph Bryan, owner of the *Richmond Times* and a former Mosby raider, had expanded the Union infantry to three thousand and the number of wagons to 150. Sheridan, for his part, never mentioned losing prisoners, cattle, horses, or mules, but did admit the loss of six wagons.

Fortunately, the disaster precipitated a Federal court of inquiry that contains the testimony and documents of assistant quartermaster J. C. Mann, the person responsible for the train. Mann noted that the train included 525 wagons carrying supplies for each of Sheridan's three infantry corps and the cavalry corps. When the attack occurred, all wagons had passed on to Winchester except the fifty wagons comprising the Cavalry Reserve Brigade train. This train, guarded by only seventy-five infantry, constituted the rear of the supply column. Mosby struck this train only and, according to Mann, burned just twenty of the fifty wagons. The undamaged wagons, most of them still loaded, were recovered after the attack and brought safety to Winchester. Mann admitted losing forty teams, or 250 mules and horses, but made no mention of the number of cattle lost. The figures, confirmed by the testimony of others, suggest that Mosby exaggerated. On the other hand, if Mosby's numbers stand, the Federals concocted and orchestrated a massive cover-up. Whatever the case, nearly ninety percent of Sheridan's train had passed to the front *before* Mosby's attack. Sheridan did not, as Mosby's biographers suggest, panic and scamper north without supplies.

Though of minimal strategic impact, Berryville demonstrated Mosby's commitment to his primary objective of slicing Sheridan's supply lines. In the three months following Berryville, the fabled guerrilla faced countless opportunities to strike Sheridan's "Achilles' heel." Targets included wagon trains in the lower Valley, ammunition cars on the Baltimore & Ohio Railroad, food and clothing transports on the Winchester & Potomac Railroad, culverts and bridges on the transportation routes, and supply depots at Harpers Ferry and Martinsburg. Yet the record reveals no successful attacks by Mosby's command against supply trains or supply bases after August 13.

Biographers of Mosby cite the famous "Greenback Raid" as an example of the Gray Ghost's success. At 2:30 A.M. on October 14, Mosby and one hundred men derailed an unguarded westbound passenger train on the B&O Railroad about eight miles northwest of Harpers Ferry. Among the frightened, German-speaking civilian passengers, the raiders found two U.S. government paymasters carrying $173,000 in greenbacks. Mosby's men seized the money, burned the train, and quickly disappeared. By 5:00 A.M., a railroad construction crew had been dispatched to the scene, and by the next day the B&O had reopened. Guerrilla John Munson labeled the Greenback Raid the "greatest piece of annoyance introduced" in Sheridan's Valley campaign. Indeed, it annoyed and embarrassed the generals responsible for protection of the B&O; compelled

Secretary of War Edwin M. Stanton to raise questions about pickets, outposts, and guards; burdened future express trains with 150-men escorts; and made sensational headlines in the newspapers. But it did not influence Sheridan's campaign against Early in any significant way.

Targets more important than passenger trains almost daily presented Mosby's command with opportunities to interdict Sheridan's supplies. For example, an average of three wagon trains per week moved south from Harpers Ferry or Martinsburg to Sheridan's front. Trains usually included five hundred wagons, but on occasion numbered more than one thousand. The excessive length and cumbersome movement of these trains (a thousand wagons stretching ten miles required four hours to pass a given point) made them especially vulnerable to guerrillas. Sheridan's white-canvas umbilical cord faced its greatest danger in late September, when his supply line extended 104 miles between Martinsburg and Harrisonburg. Yet Mosby's command failed to interrupt even one train. Rations, ammunition, and clothing in thousands of wagons moved unimpeded to Sheridan's army far advanced into enemy territory. Meanwhile, captured prisoners, armaments, and livestock from Early's army trudged steadily north for distribution at Harpers Ferry and Martinsburg. The twin Confederate disasters at Third Winchester and Fisher's Hill, for example, brought a wagon train to Martinsburg carrying seven thousand rebel small arms, ten pieces of Confederate artillery, five C. S. A. caissons, and eighty prisoners. Interception of this captured booty would have bolstered Confederate fortunes considerably, but Mosby mounted no effort.

Confederate prisoners presented additional opportunities for Mosby and his men. By the end of September, 3,250 unwounded prisoners—the equivalent of more than a full Confederate division—had arrived at Harpers Ferry without incident. Where was Mosby? "Silently we prayed that Mosby might make a dash and rescue us," recalled one depressed prisoner. "All night long we vainly listened for the clatter of hoofs of Mosby's troopers. But, alas! Mosby did not come."

Even the B&O Railroad, Sheridan's primary life-support system, escaped Mosby's expected terror. With the exception of the Greenback Raid, which had no impact on Sheridan's operations, the Gray Ghost failed to inflict damage to the line. Supplies arrived daily at Harpers Ferry and Martinsburg, and civilian travel and business increased on the previously troubled railroad. The B&O prospered during Sheridan's campaign, earning one dollar for each soldier it transported and additional income from military tonnage. On September 22, the day Sheridan routed Early at Fisher's Hill, the B&O delivered at Harpers Ferry 4,924 reinforcements, enough to replace the bulk of Sheridan's losses at Third Winchester and Fisher's Hill.

Mosby thus failed to disrupt Sheridan's wagon trains, interrupt essential railroad traffic, recover captured Confederates, and execute his primary objective of severing the enemy's supplies. In view of his apparent opportunity, why did Mosby falter? Sheridan's structural organization offers one reason. A week after his arrival in the Valley, Sheridan assigned Brigadier General John D. Stevenson to command the Military District of Harpers Ferry. Competent, aggressive, and sometimes arrogant, the forty-four-year-old, mustachioed Virginian understood his mission perfectly: "The loss of one train by a careless officer would defeat a campaign." From his headquarters at Harpers Ferry, Stevenson answered directly to Sheridan, overseeing all supply logistics, including arrivals and departures of trains, strength of escorts and procedures for their deployment, and operations of depots at the Ferry and at distribution centers at Martinsburg and Winchester. Stevenson viewed Sheridan's rear as his front, and his singular coordination of supply activities plugged many Federal holes and eliminated many potential targets.

Counterintelligence measures instituted by Sheridan, both military and civilian, also impaired Mosby's ability to prey on Yankee supplies. Jessie Scouts, or Union spies dressed in Confederate uniforms, often gleaned information from unsuspecting victims through casual conversations. "They [brought] me almost every day intelligence from within [Confederate] lines," Sheridan boasted. Though never large in numbers, the Jessies made it difficult to distinguish friend from foe and inserted a level of mistrust into Rebel ranks.

Complementing Sheridan's surreptitious scouts was Captain Richard Blazer's company of one hundred hand-picked men. Armed with Spencer repeaters and ordered by Sheridan "to clean out Mosby's gang," Blazer's command did nothing but hunt for John Singleton Mosby. Blazer's constant hounding often forced the Gray Ghost to seek refuge rather than scout for missions, thus limiting Mosby's knowledge of vulnerable Federal targets. Annoyed and frustrated by Blazer, partisan John Scott recalled: "[Blazer] appeared to be ever in the saddle, and was constantly turning up where he was least expected and least desired." Scott concluded that Mosby and Blazer could not long inhabit opposite sides of the Blue Ridge, and Scott proved correct—Mosby's men eventually annihilated Blazer's command at Myerstown, but not until November 18, nearly one month after the Valley campaign had ended with Sheridan's climatic victory at Cedar Creek.

Sheridan also adapted measures to control civilians friendly to Mosby. Union authorities realized that "non-combatants" provided Mosby with hundreds of pairs of eyes and ears to monitor Federal operatives. In addition, civilians in "Mosby's Confederacy" fed the partisans and provided shelter from incessant Federal pursuers. "Robin Hood concealed his men in the solitudes of Sherwood Forest," observed a Mosby ranger. "Marion took refuge in the inaccessible swamps of Carolina . . . but Mosby, in an open country, finds security in dispersion among a friendly and chivalrous people." As John Munson fondly recalled, "Every man in the command had some special farm he could call his home."

To eradicate this enemy without uniforms, the Federals implemented stringent policies that included the detention of civilians. The Berryville wagon train raid of August 13 elicited the first emotional response. "The families of most of Mosby's men are known and can be collected," an irritated U. S. Grant informed Sheridan three days after the raid. "I think they should be taken and kept at Fort McHenry, or some secure

place, as hostages for the good conduct of Mosby and his men."
Sheridan subsequently responded on August 19 with an order
to arrest all "able bodied male citizens under the age of fifty
who may be suspected of aiding, assisting, or belonging to gue-
rilla bands now infesting the country." Seven weeks later, after
guerrilla attacks had killed Sheridan's chief engineer, chief
medical inspector, and chief quartermaster in an eight-day period, an angry Sheridan announced: "I know of no way to ex-
terminate [guerrillas] except to burn out the whole country
and let the people go North or South." Sheridan best implemented this policy in Loudoun County, a part of Mosby's
Confederacy, in the first days of December, letting the populace know "there is a God in Israel." The Union commander
informed Washington that the "people are beginning to see
that [Mosby] does not injure me a great deal, but causes a loss
to them of all they have spent their lives in accumulating."
Although Sheridan's policy of intimidation, imprisonment,
destruction, and hardship never broke the will of Mosby's
civilian supporters, the burdens of poverty minimized civilian
intelligence-gathering and disarmed one of Mosby's most powerful weapons.

Another factor that contributed to Mosby's noninterdiction
of supplies was his untimely absence from command. A
Yankee bullet ricocheted off Mosby's pistol into his groin on
the evening of September 14 near Falls Church. The Federals
who ambushed Mosby along the Centreville Road failed to
capture the wounded partisan, but he remained out of action
for two crucial weeks. During Mosby's absence, Sheridan
whipped Early at Third Winchester and Fisher's Hill, then pursued the routed Confederates as far south as Port Republic and
Staunton. "When I was wounded," Mosby subsequently wrote,
"Sheridan's line of communication was not over ten miles in
length and difficult to strike. Now it was 150 [sic] miles long
and assailable in a hundred places, [yet] comparatively little
[was] done."

Mosby attributed the ineffectiveness of his command to the
"jealousy of the officers." Competition among Mosby's lieutenants for the glory and honor of the most successful raid and

biggest booty sometimes superseded the needs of the service. Thus, instead of cooperating during Mosby's absence, company commanders searched for their own prey. Several leaders, including two captains and a major, used Mosby's absence as an opportunity to take furloughs. Mosby believed that "the command had never before had such an opportunity to strike a heavy blow"; without his leadership, however, the opportunity passed.

Federal escorts also inhibited Mosby's strikes. To insure adequate protection for his wagon trains, Sheridan insisted on deploying veterans for this duty. "It would take more than a hundred days to teach men how to successfully encounter Mosby," observed one New York cavalryman. Sheridan called upon a tested brigade of infantry from the Nineteenth Corps to protect his line of supplies. Boasting nearly eighteen hundred men in its four New York regiments and the ranks of the 30th Maine, the Third Brigade of the First Division received its initial escort assignment on August 14. Under the capable command of Colonel Leonard D. H. Currie, the brigade specialized in opposing Mosby, learning the roads, woods, and dark corners most favorable for guerrilla attacks. As a result of its familiarity with terrain and its omnipresent vigilance, Currie's brigade never faltered, escorting—without mishap in ten weeks—seventeen trains to and from the front.

Sheridan never credited Currie for his outstanding performance. Instead, in his clouded postwar memoirs the general complimented Mosby by redeploying thousands to the Federal rear. "The difference in strength between the two armies was considerably in my favor," wrote Sheridan, "but the conditions attending my situation in a hostile region necessitated so much detached service . . . that my excess in numbers was almost cancelled." Commenting on this egregious assessment in an 1899 article in the *Richmond Times*, Mosby expressed gratification at "the highest tribute ever paid to the efficiency of my command."

The facts support neither Sheridan's nor Mosby's memories. The record reveals post commanders at Harpers Ferry, Martinsburg, and Winchester usually scrambling for adequate escorts. General Stevenson at Harpers Ferry sounded the first alarm when he informed Sheridan on September 21 that the "supply trains and all army trains [some one thousand wagons] left here last night. I am now without troops for escorts of any kind, having sent forward everything." After rushing another train toward the front on the twenty-second under escort of remounted cavalry, Stevenson nearly panicked: "My great difficulty is escorts. Have sent forward every soldier that can be used at this post; nothing left except my necessary guards." Insufficient escorts once detained a wagon train scheduled to resupply Sheridan at Harrisonburg. Colonel Oliver Edwards, commander at Winchester, refused to permit the 250 wagons to move south without a two-thousand-man escort. When Stevenson, Edwards's superior, learned of the train's detention he abruptly insisted that there "must be no delay in sending forward trains if it takes every man. . . . Supplies must go forward, even though your post may be skinned down to the smallest possible number." Stevenson became so desperate for escorts, he informed Sheridan on October 5 that he had "3,000 convalescents, stragglers, recruits, etc., armed, equipped, and properly organized for the next train."

Stevenson's syphoning of troops to accompany trains created another problem by dangerously exposing Federal bases to guerrilla attack. Martinsburg commandant Brigadier General Thomas Neill felt such alarm at his defenseless depot that he carried his anxieties directly to the War Department. "I do not consider my post safe," he wired Secretary Stanton on September 30, "unless I have stronger force to protect the large amount of Government property rapidly accumulating here." Neill requested one regiment of cavalry and two of infantry for duty at Martinsburg, but Secretary Stanton dismissed the brigadier's clamor for troops with a terse "I know of none."

Stevenson also recognized the vulnerability of Sheridan's supply depots. "I have depleted [this] post to the lowest possible point," he told Sheridan on October 9. "I have no infantry proper." One week later, after noting the return of Currie's brigade to the front, the reassignment of two regiments to western Virginia, and the forthcoming expiration of three 100-days' organizations (about four thousand men in all), a desperate Stevenson exclaimed that in "case of an attack upon [Harpers Ferry] I could not muster 1,000 trusty soldiers." The frustrated supply officer then reminded Sheridan that when "you reflect upon the fact that Martinsburg and a railroad line of fifty miles have been added to my responsibilities . . . you will not accuse me of false clamor." Stevenson concluded by warning, "I cannot consider my force sufficient either for defense if attacked or for offense against the forces of the enemy [Mosby] to your rear."

These contemporary revelations refute Sheridan's assertion that he pulled thousands of combat troops from his front to protect supplies in his rear. At most, five thousand Federals—about twelve percent of Sheridan's strength in the Shenandoah—protected Northern lifelines in the Valley. Mosby could argue with justifiable pride that he tied up Yankees ten times his own strength; however, Sheridan had so many men that the absence of detached Union soldiers made little difference on battlefields in the Valley.

Although Mosby failed to strike Sheridan's weakly guarded bases, interrupt Yankee supply lines, or isolate the Union army, the Gray Ghost claimed success with his third objective—the disruption of Sheridan's communications. Union couriers riding to and from the front provided perfect targets. Despite cavalry escorts, couriers and their guards seldom matched Mosby's numbers, and guerrillas persistently harassed them. "Both of my last courier parties were attacked," Stevenson wired Secretary of War Stanton on September 27. "Message No. 31 was sent by both parties, and both have failed . . . I doubt if we shall be able to get any dispatches through without sending much larger body of cavalry than I can get hold of."

Disruption of couriers reached its climax during the first week of October with Sheridan's front south of Harrisonburg. Messages now traveled more than one hundred miles to and from the commanding general, and as Colonel Edwards at Winchester observed, "Escorts with dispatches have to cut their way through, and generally lose half of their men." Interruptions became so severe that the secretary of war complained of not being properly informed of events at the front. On October 7, Sheridan acknowledged his inability "to communicate more frequently on account of the operations of guerrillas in my rear."

Capture of one of these messages led Mosby to proclaim his greatest exploit against Sheridan. During the last week of September, an intercepted dispatch informed the guerrilla commander of Federal intentions to rebuild the Manassas Gap Railroad. The reconstructed line, which ran through the heart of Mosby's Confederacy, would serve as the initial leg in the transfer of most of Sheridan's army back to Grant. Although still recovering from his September 14 wound, Mosby returned to his command on the twenty-ninth. Six days later, he attacked Union railroad builders at Salem. "We never thought much of the Salem fight as mere *tactical* operation," a satisfied Mosby wrote thirty-five years after the war, "but strategically it was the most important thing we ever did. But for our success there Richmond would have fallen in a week."

Mosby's audacious assertion assumes that the Manassas Gap Railroad was critical in Sheridan's plan to transfer his army to Petersburg. The record reveals otherwise. Grant first suggested opening the Manassas Gap line in a letter to Halleck on September 22. "Old Brains" ordered repair of the railroad ten days later, but Sheridan never acquiesced. "I would have preferred sending troops to you by the Baltimore and Ohio Railroad," Sheridan observed to the commanding general on October 7. "It would have been the quickest and most concealed way of sending them."

Despite Sheridan's reservations and Mosby's persistent strikes, work continued on the Manassas Gap line until October 11, when Sheridan announced his intention to *march* the Sixth Corps to Alexandria. "To transport the corps will break up its organization," Sheridan insisted to Halleck, "and the shipment of artillery, horses, trains, and officers' traps will involve so much trouble and delay, that no time will be gained [via the railroad]." Sheridan concluded, "All things duly considered, I

would advise the march." With other options available for
Sheridan to unite his army with Grant's, Confederate activity
along the Manassas Gap line clearly did not save Richmond.
Mosby's presence did affect Sheridan's route to Richmond.
Following the pursuit of Early's defeated army south of
Harrisonburg, Grant wanted Sheridan to cross over the Blue
Ridge, strike supply and hospital centers at Charlottesville and
Gordonsville, sever the Virginia Central Railroad, and threaten
Richmond from the back door. Sheridan stubbornly rejected
this strategy, declaring it "impracticable." Apprising Grant
that "it is no easy matter to pass these mountain gaps," he
suggested the Confederates would fortify Charlottesville and
Gordonsville, rendering them impossible to take "without the
expenditure of a largely superior force to keep open the line
of communication." Without mentioning Mosby by name,
Sheridan declared that guerrillas would be a problem, requiring
an entire corps to protect either the Orange & Alexandria
Railroad or the Manassas Gap line, his crucial supply routes
for the operation. "My judgement is that it would be best to
terminate this campaign," stated Sheridan in summary, "by
the destruction of the crops, etc., in this valley, and [then]
transfer the troops to the army operating against Richmond."
Largely due to the threat posed by Mosby, Sheridan thus rec-
ommended a retrograde movement and transfer out of the
Valley rather than an advance east of the Blue Ridge.

Sheridan began withdrawing north from Harrisonburg on
October 6, prompting Mosby to proclaim thirty years after
the war that his command had "prevented" Sheridan from following up his victories over Early and thereby preserved "for
six months the life of the Confederacy." This egocentric
declaration failed to recognize the unfinished business that
kept Sheridan in the Valley. Little Phil considered the Valley,
not the Virginia Central Railroad towns coveted by Grant, his
primary military target. For three years the lush Shenandoah
had provided Confederate soldiers with thousands of tons
of food. In Sheridan's opinion, laying waste to this Rebel
breadbasket was tantamount to the disruption of the Central
railroad. "The destruction of the grain and forage from here

will be a terrible blow to them," Sheridan assured Grant. "I will go on and clean out the Valley."

On the morning of October 6, as the Union infantry slowly withdrew down the Valley Pike, Sheridan's cavalry methodically burned the Valley from Harrisonburg to Woodstock. Thirty-six hours later, smoldering ashes littered the smoky landscape. The Federals had burned more than two thousand barns filled with freshly harvested wheat and hay; destroyed more than seventy mills loaded with flour and wheat; slaughtered three thousand sheep; and driven north with the army more than four thousand head of stock. "The people here are getting sick of war," Sheridan explained to Grant. "Heretofore they have had no reason to complain, because they have been living in great abundance." By the time the Federals settled at Cedar Creek on October 10, Sheridan had completed his mission in the Valley: "From Winchester up to Staunton, ninety-two miles, [there is] little in it for man or beast."

With the Valley destroyed and no apparent sign of the enemy in his front, Sheridan commenced transferring a portion of his army to Grant. On October 11, the Sixth Corps reached Front Royal with orders to begin marching to Alexandria on the twelfth. These troops failed to reach Alexandria, but not because of any action by Mosby. Early's sudden and unexpected resurgence forced Sheridan to recall the Sixth Corps to Cedar Creek. Sheridan's subsequent victory there on October 19 crushed the Confederate army; however, Sheridan retained his full strength in the Shenandoah until the first week of December. Hence the additional six weeks that the Sixth Corps spent in the Valley—and the resulting temporary Confederate respite at Richmond—must be credited to Jubal Early rather than to Mosby.

Despite Mosby's failure to disrupt the supply lines and strategy of Sheridan in the Valley (not to mention his failure to prolong the life of the Confederacy by six months), his partisans constituted an irritation to the Union invaders. Villified by the Yankees as a "quasi-military pest," Mosby operated against Federal cavalry, pickets, railroads, and couriers, both annoying and embarrassing Union authorities. However, while Mosby's activities sometimes drew blood, they never inflicted a major wound.

To Mosby's credit, one point remains unchallenged: "But few men in the South could have commanded successfully a separate detachment, in the rear of an opposing army and so near the border of hostilities, as long as [Mosby] did without losing his entire command." Grant's postwar accolade aptly summarizes Mosby's most significant achievement against Sheridan; against odds stacked heavily against him, Mosby depended upon his personal skill, daring, and bravery to survive in the uneven match. "There was a great stake to be won," the Gray Ghost concluded, "and I resolved to play a bold game to win it." Mosby did indeed play boldly in the Shenandoah against Sheridan—and lost.

Bibliographic Note

The printed literature on the 1864 Valley campaign is modest in comparison to that devoted to more famous campaigns such as Gettysburg or Antietam, but it nonetheless includes works that offer something for a wide spectrum of students. Anyone wishing to see what the participants themselves wrote at the time should start with the U.S. War Department's *The War of the Rebellion: A Compilation of the Official Records of the Union and Confederate Armies* (127 vols., index, and atlas; Washington, D.C., 1880–1901). This massive set, usually referred to as the *Official Records* or the *OR*, contains reports, correspondence, orders of battle, and maps relating to every phase of the campaign. Series 1, volume 37, parts 1 and 2 (two large volumes) cover Early's operations from June through the first days of August; series 1, volume 43, parts 1 and 2 (another brace of thick tomes) takes the campaign from early August through December 1864. No other published source approaches the *Official Records* in size or scope, though readers should always keep in mind that the reports often portray events in a self-serving manner. Two useful collections of early articles are Clarence Clough Buel and Robert Underwood Johnson, eds., *Battles and Leaders of the Civil War* (4 vols.; New York, 1887 [reprinted several times]), and Military Historical Society of Massachusetts, *Papers*, vol. 6, *The Shenandoah Campaigns of 1862 and 1864 and the Appomattox Campaign 1865* (1907; reprint, Wilmington, N.C., 1989). Even more than the *Official Records*, the articles in these sets must be used with an eye toward potential bias.

The best general treatment of the decisive phase of the campaign is Jeffry D. Wert's *From Winchester to Cedar Creek: The Shenandoah Campaign of 1864* (Carlisle, Pa., 1987). Scholarly and well-written, Wert's narrative provides an even-handed analysis of both Early and Sheridan. A pair of modern studies explores the initial phase of Early's operations—*Jubal's Raid: General Early's Famous Attack on Washington in 1864* (New York, 1960) by Frank E. Vandiver, and

Jubal Early's Raid on Washington, 1864 (Baltimore, 1989) by B. F. Cooling. Vandiver's is the more gracefully written of the two, Cooling's the more deeply researched. On the Battle of the Monocacy, see Glenn H. Worthington, *Fighting for Time: The Battle That Saved Washington and Mayhap the Union* (1932; reprint, Shippensburg, Pa., 1985). A profusely illustrated—though often untrustworthy—popular discussion of the entire campaign is Edward J. Stackpole, *Sheridan in the Shenandoah: Jubal Early's Nemesis* (Harrisburg, Pa., 1961). For a better mix of illustrative material and text, readers should consult Thomas A. Lewis and the Editors of Time-Life Books, *The Shenandoah in Flames: The Valley Campaign of 1864* (Alexandria, Va., 1987). Older volumes that retain value include George E. Pond, *The Shenandoah Valley in 1864* (1883; reprint, Wilmington, N.C., 1989, with an introduction by Jeffry D. Wert), which views the action from a largely Northern perspective; Henry A. Du Pont, *The Campaign of 1864 in the Valley of Virginia and the Expedition to Lynchburg* (New York, 1925), a combination of analysis and personal reminiscence by an artillerist under Sheridan; and Sanford C. Kellogg, *The Shenandoah Valley and Virginia, 1861 to 1865: A War Study* (New York, 1903), a general treatment of the Valley during the war that allots a third of its text to 1864.

Neither Sheridan nor Early has been the subject of a satisfactory biography; the standard life of Early is Millard K. Bushong's openly appreciative *Old Jube: A Biography of General Jubal A. Early* (Boyce, Va., 1955), while the best of a mediocre lot on Sheridan is Henry E. Davies's *General Sheridan* (New York, 1894). A hostile view of the Federal chief may be found in Raoul S. Naroll, "Sheridan and Cedar Creek: A Reappraisal," in Editors of Military Affairs, *Military Analysis of the Civil War* (Millwood, N.Y., 1977). Ralph Lowell Eckert's *John Brown Gordon: Soldier, Southerner, American* (Baton Rouge, 1989), Gary W. Gallagher's *Stephen Dodson Ramseur: Lee's Gallant General* (Chapel Hill, 1985), and Virgil Carrington Jones's *Ranger Mosby* (Chapel Hill, 1944) explore the roles of three key Confederate figures in the Valley. On the Federal side, T. Harry Williams's *Hayes of the Twenty-third: The Civil War Volunteer Officer* (New York, 1965) is superb; Edward W. Emerson's *The Life and Letters of Charles Russell Lowell* (Boston, 1907) often compelling; Gregory J. W. Irwin's *Custer Victorious: The Civil War Battles of General George Armstrong Custer* (Rutherford, Madison, and Teaneck, N.J., 1983) and Don E. Alberts's *Brandy Station to Manila Bay: A Biography of General Wesley Merritt* (Austin, Tex., 1980) less enlightening but still of value.

Each of the army commanders wrote a long reminiscence. Sheridan's *Personal Memoirs* (2 volumes; New York, 1888) and Early's *Lieutenant General Jubal Anderson Early C.S.A., Autobiographical Sketch and Narrative of the War Between the States* (1912; reprint, Wilmington, N.C., 1989, with an introduction by Gary W. Gallagher) contain scant recognition of any redeeming feature in the other's military character, though Early's is the more honest and useful work. Other illuminating books by veterans of the campaign include Jedediah Hotchkiss's indispensable *Make Me a Map of the Valley: The Civil War Journal of Stonewall Jackson's Topographer* (edited by Archie P. McDonald, Dallas, 1973); George Crook's blunt *General George Crook: His Autobiography* (edited by Martin F. Schmitt, Norman, Okla., 1946); John S. Mosby's alternately revealing and frustrating *The Memoirs of Colonel John S. Mosby* (1917; reprint Bloomington, Ind., 1959, with an introduction by Virgil Carrington Jones); John Scott's detailed *Partisan Life with Col. John S. Mosby* (1867; reprint, Gaithersburg, Md., 1985); John W. Munson's charming *Reminiscences of a Mosby Guerrilla* (1906; reprint, Washington, D.C., 1983); and George B. Sanford's *Fighting Rebels and Redskins: Experiences in Army Life of Colonel George B. Sanford, 1861–1892* (edited by E. R. Hagerman, Norman, Okla., 1969). John B. Gordon's widely quoted *Reminiscences of the Civil War* (1903; reprint, Dayton, Ohio, 1985) is colorful but filled with exaggerations and apocryphal incidents, while Henry Kyd Douglas's *I Rode with Stonewall* (Chapel Hill, 1940) matches Gordon's color and manages a closer brush with veracity.

Three basic unit histories are Frank M. Myers's *The Comanches: A History of White's Battalion, Virginia Cavalry, Laurel Brig., Hampton Div., A.N.V., C.S.A.* (1871; reprint, Gaithersburg, Md., 1987, with an introduction by Lee A. Wallace, Jr.); Richard B. Irwin's *History of the Nineteenth Army Corps* (1892; reprint, Baton Rouge, La., 1985, with an introduction by Lawrence L. Hewitt); and Aldace F. Walker's *The Vermont Brigade in the Shenandoah Valley, 1864* (Burlington, Vt., 1869). The best study of Mosby's partisans during the 1864 Valley Campaign is Jeffry D. Wert, *Mosby's Rangers* (New York, 1990). Stephen Z. Starr does full justice to Sheridan's powerful mounted arm in *The Union Cavalry in the Civil War,* vol. 2, *The War in the East from Gettysburg to Appomattox, 1863–1865* (Baton Rouge, La., 1981).

In a class by itself is James E. Taylor, *The James E. Taylor Sketchbook: With Sheridan Up the Shenandoah Valley in 1864, Leaves from a Special Artist's Sketch Book and Diary* (edited by Dennis E. Frye, Martin F. Graham, and George F. Skoch, Dayton, Ohio, 1989). A special artist for *Frank Leslie's Illustrated Newspaper*, Taylor accompanied the Federal army in the Valley, sketching as he went. After the war, he gathered his wartime sketches and written impressions, added later drawings, and produced a mammoth illustrated account of the 1864 Valley campaign. Because of its depiction of the places and people who figured in the operations, it serves as a perfect companion to other accounts of the action.

Two multivolume histories merit inclusion on a short list of books relating to the 1864 Valley campaign. Douglas Southall Freeman's *Lee's Lieutenants: A Study in Command* (3 vols.; New York, 1942–44) traces Early's movements and battles in some detail. Based on wide research and marked by great narrative power, Freeman's classic study commands attention from all serious readers. Another brilliantly written trilogy is Shelby Foote's *The Civil War: A Narrative* (New York, 1958–74), the third volume of which addresses events in the Shenandoah Valley during 1864.

Readers may be intrigued by aspects of the 1864 Valley campaign not covered sufficiently by these titles. In that case, they should peruse the notes and bibliographies of these books for leads about where else they might look.

Index

Contributors

DENNIS E. FRYE is the historian at Harpers Ferry National Historic Park. A graduate of Shepherd College, he is active as a tour leader, lecturer, and author on subjects relating to the era of the Civil War. His publications include *Second Virginia Infantry* and *Twelfth Virginia Cavalry* in the "Virginia Regimental Histories Series." He is currently writing a book on Stonewall Jackson's siege of Harpers Ferry.

GARY W. GALLAGHER is head of the Department of History at Pennsylvania State University. He has published widely on the Civil War, including *Stephen Dodson Ramseur: Lee's Gallant General, Fighting for the Confederacy: The Personal Recollections of General Edward Porter Alexander,* and *Antietam: Essays on the 1862 Maryland Campaign.* He is presently completing a biography of Jubal A. Early.

A. WILSON GREENE holds degrees in American history from Florida State University and Louisiana State University. An active lecturer and author, he is executive director of the Association for the Preservation of Civil War Sites. He has written articles for a variety of historical journals as well as *J. Horace Lacy: The Most Dangerous Rebel of the County.* His *Whatever You Resolve to Be: Essays on Stonewall Jackson* will be published in 1991.

ROBERT K. KRICK was raised and educated in northern California and has lived in Virginia for two decades. He is the author of eight books on Confederate history, among them *Lee's Colonels, Parker's Virginia Battery,* and *Stonewall Jackson at Cedar Mountain.* His latest project is a study of the final phase of Jackson's Valley campaign.

JEFFRY D. WERT is a Civil War historian and teacher who lives in Centre Hall, Pennsylvania. The author of *From Winchester to Cedar Creek: The Shenandoah Valley Campaign of 1864, Mosby's Rangers,* and dozens of articles, he is at work on a major study of James Longstreet's career as a Confederate officer.